Suggested Year Plan

Most schools begin in late August or early September, leaving ~30 weeks t[illegible] or review before the exam. Some books, however, such as Stearns and Bentley, have more than ~30 chapters, [illegible] to do 'a chapter a week' and still have time for review at the end. With 23 chapters, however, the Strayer text more than fits the bill scheduling-wise, especially if you want to enjoy the semblance of military-style class structure. What follows is the book's contents, and a blast from the past of how the AP World History course was ordered when it was young.

	Strayer 3rd Ed. (2015) ***Weekly Breakdown***	**McNeill's *A World History* (1967) ***Flashback*****
Chapter 1	First People, First Farmers	In the Beginning
Chapter 2	First Civilizations	Diffusion of Civilization: First Phase
Chapter 3	State and Empire	Cosmopolitanism in the Middle East
Chapter 4	Culture and Religion	Definition of Indian Civilization
Chapter 5	Society and Inequality	Definition of Greek Civilization
Chapter 6	Commonalities and Variations	Definition of Chinese Civilization
Chapter 7	Commerce and Culture	Changes in the Barbarian World
Chapter 8	China and the World	Flowering of Greek Civilization
Chapter 9	The Worlds of Islam	Spread of Hellenistic Civilization
Chapter 10	The Worlds of Christendom	Flowering of Indian Civilization
Chapter 11	Pastoral Peoples	Barbarian Invasions and Civilized Response
Chapter 12	The Worlds of the 15th Century	Rise of Islam
Chapter 13	Political Transformations	China, India and Europe A.D. 600-1000
Chapter 14	Economic Transformations	Turkish and Mongol Conquests
Chapter 15	Cultural Transformations	Medieval Europe and Japan 1000-1500
Chapter 16	Atlantic Revolutions	Fringes of the Civilized World to 1500
Chapter 17	Revolutions of Industrialization	The Great Discoveries and Consequences
Chapter 18	Colonial Encounters in the East	Europe's Self-Transformation 1500-1648
Chapter 19	Empires in Collision	Europe's Outliers: Russia and America
Chapter 20	Collapse at the Center	Realm of Islam and Subject Communities
Chapter 21	Rise and Fall of World Communism	The Far East 1500-1750
Chapter 22	The End of Empire	The Old Regime in Europe 1648-1789
Chapter 23	Capitalism and Culture	Asian Reactions to the Old Regime
Chapter 24	--	Industry's Transformation of the West
Chapter 25	--	Non-Western World since 1850
Chapter 26	--	Western World since 1917

Suggested Weekly Plan

Manic Moon Day

It is recommended that students have a lecture overview of the key points in each chapter, take notes, and discuss the concepts involved. Even though teachers are discouraged in some parts of the country from lecturing, the speed of the AP* World History course necessitates some direct teacher-student transmission of content. Perhaps participation grades could be assigned for notes? Conversely, the chapter assignment forms could be used as a guide during the discussion. As you read, note the significance of contents in the chapter.

Textbook Tiw's Day

Most school districts encourage pair or group work. This can be used to positive effect if students mine the textbook (or a review book) in class and either jigsaw the chapter, presenting their take on part of the whole, or jointly venture to find the answers to the specific problems in history. Groups could take part of each chapter assignment and report.

Writing Woden's Day

The AP* World History curriculum is reading and writing intensive, and a good way to build up the key thinking processes helpful in expressing oneself in writing is to brainstorm and diagram solutions to mini-FRQs appropriate to each chapter. Another helpful way to do writings is good old-fashioned reading comprehension, and as many teachers know, the content of the passages is key to student growth and success. If it ain't interesting, you might as well be pulling teeth at the dentist's office. Luckily, World History has a great potential interest value. If you find the current materials helpful and of high enough quality, you may want to obtain the companion volume to this book, *Tamm's Textbook Tools Coursepak Series B: Reading Shorts, Writings and Online Activities*, on *Amazon.com* or another platform.

Technetronic Thor's Day

Many AP* teachers try to bring in technology to the classroom, whether in the form of a laptop cart, or by taking students to a media lab. Increasingly, students are just using their mobile devices. *Kahoot.it* is now popular as a Jeopardy-style review game, joining *Quizlet* and a vast number of other review materials available online. A good directory to websites usable with AP World History classes, including the Strayer textbook site with history activities, is located at Antarcticaedu.com/Hst.htm. Included in the addendum to this volume is a Crash Course viewer response sheet that can be given as homework on Thursday nights, or completed as an in-class review assignment.

Fantastic Frija's Day

It is suggested that students take a 25-50-question test once a week. That means some chapters will probably have to be doubled up. A 35 min. period should be reserved in class- or in some cases out depending on how nice you are- to do these weekly tests. If this happens on Friday, it is recommended students take home the chapter assignments or at least part of them for homework. Doing the vocab itself is a good way to introduce the new chapter.

Now let's get down to business!

Nothing like a first impression

Pic 10: Art can be an expression of aspects of the artist's inner life (or imagination), but what does it mean here that this image, by the San of Southern Africa, is a depiction of the 'outer' life?

Hunter-gatherers

(*Nota Bene: The best way to gain a grasp of the vocab is to summarize the term in the context of its importance in the chapter, in this case, in the 'Eyewitness' story*)

Paleolithic

Neolithic

Homo sapiens

Note some factors that went into the 'human revolution':

Make a list of tools early humans invented and made use of?

Blombos Cave

Ice Age

Cave art

Venus figurines

Aboriginal Australians

Dreamtime

Pic 15: Early Australians had a unique style of painting called the Aboriginal ________________style. What characteristics does it have?

Map 16: Humans migrated to almost all parts of the world in prehistoric times. List the six inhabited continents in the order they were populated with the years in parentheses:

Pituri

Describe the concept of *diffusion* in your own words:

Clovis point

Map 19: Start at the Philippines and list the South Pacific island chains and places in the order in which people colonized them (remember, B.C.E. is B.C. and C.E. is A.D.):

Moa

Kinship

The population density during Paleolithic times was very *a. dense* *b. sparse* compared with now.

The Toba Catastrophe is the name of the volcanic eruption the authors are talking about that occurred on Sumatra, which, along with Borneo and Java, are the major Spice Islands.

What do scholars speculate the population of the world dropped to after that eruption?

Is the number you obtained for the previous question a greater or lesser number of people worldwide than the city or town you live in?

Historians have speculated that during the Paleolithic Era, human societies were freer and more equal than in any future society, including ours. What are their main points as to why?

Pic 21: Are you 'envious' of the lifestyle of hunter-gatherers as the authors think Captain Cook was? Why or why not?

Describe the role of *shamans* in early belief systems:

Most non-African human beings have between 2-4 percent Neanderthal DNA. Both *Homo sapiens sapiens* (us) and *Homo sapiens neanderthalensis* (sort of us) are classified as *hominid.* Hominids are:

a. cetaceans *b. primates*

which are *a. mammals* *b. amphibians*

| Pic 23: Prehistoric art takes two major | forms. Large animals were painted for | good luck on the life-and-death hunt, | and what about life-and-death is present | in the Venus figurines like this one?

Trance dance

'Ceremonial space'

Animism

Snapshot 24: According to this chart, what percentage of all humans who have ever lived have lived in the last 200 years (10 generations, or else 7 'great grandparents' ago):

| Describe what is happening | regarding life expectancy:

Global warming

What did the process of 'settling down,' also known as the Neolithic revolution, mean for people as a lifestyle change?

Zooming In 26: After reading the selection, answer the analysis questions that follow:

1)

2)

Neolithic Era

Agricultural Revolution

Animal domestication

How does the term 'intensification' fit into the ongoing trend towards farming and animal domestication?

Map 30: Plant and animal domestication – what kinds of crops did peoples around the world begin harvesting during the Neolithic Transition, also known as the Agricultural Revolution (you know, the 'revolution' that took 4000 years)! It is like when a snail starts going across your driveway, it probably seems like a revolution to the snail when it actually gets to the other side. What specific animals did people bring into their communities (farms animals and 'pets' count), and what plants did they domesticate?

	ANIMALS	**PLANTS**
SOUTHWEST ASIA (FERTILE CRESCENT)		
SOUTHWEST STEPPES (INDO-EUROPEANS)		
CENTRAL ASIA		
EAST ASIA		
SOUTHEAST ASIA		
NEW GUINEA		
SAHARAN AFRICA		
SUDANIC AFRICA		
WEST AFRICA		
EASTERN NORTH AMERICA		
MESOAMERICA		
ANDEAN REGION		
AMAZON VALLEY		

Horticulture

Note the modern day countries that make up the Fertile Crescent: | This relatively uncommon fruit is thought to be the very first cultivated crop:

Map 33: The two rivers that flow through the Fertile Crescent are: | The mountain chain separating it from Persia are the:

The Eastern Hemisphere had many more 'valuable' domesticated animals than the Americas did. Jared Diamond of UCLA believes that is one reason there was such a huge power disparity when the inevitable meeting of the two hemispheres occurred after Columbus' 1492 voyage. What do the authors state the Native Americans lacked due to this dearth in domestic animals?

Pic 35: If you wanted to visit the site of the discovery of these statues, which country would you fly to? | How did agricultural techniques diffuse from their hearths?

Map 37: Without drawing the whole continent, draw and label the rivers of Africa in their general location, from Niger to Orange, and include Lake Victoria and Lake Chad. Then, draw the arrows following the **Bantu migrations** from the Niger past the Congo and to the Zambezi and Orange:

Zooming In 38: After reading the selection, answer the analysis questions that follow:

1)

2)

3)

Animal domestication came at a price. List some of the disease that humans were exposed to in greater numbers due to their closeness to the animals in question:

____

Xian ____

Banpo village ____

Pic 40: Do you think this Nok sculpture from West Africa is really 'thinking'- or did modern archeologists put their own ideas into the name?

____

What do you think the authors mean when they say alcoholic beverages were both a blessing and a curse for humanity?

____

Pastoralism ____

Judging by the Biblical story of Cain and Abel, which was the more respected lifestyle to the Israelites?

____

Pic 42: In this cave painting, what do the circles represent?

____

This image depicts a scene most related to

a. hunting *b. animal husbandry*

Note some examples of how a social order began to appear at Catalhuyuk:

____

'Title societies' ____

Pic 45: Sketch out the broad outlines of Cahokia at right, and Be sure to include the central building, huts, avenues, etc.:

Which large U.S. city is nearest the Cahokia earthen mound today? ____

Under the dome of the sky, over endless fields, it is time to walk the paths of the ancestors

Pic 58: These people helped manage the political and economic apparatus of Egypt, among the oldest of world civilizations. Do you agree with the Mother Nature Network from the 1960s, Huck Finn and Henry David Thoreau that the 'weight of civilization' can be overbearing? In other words, what would you give up for 'freedom from civilization'? Electricity? Running water? Nothing?

Civilization

Note some of the attributes of civilization:

How was the political organization of Sumer, the earliest civilization in Mesopotamia, different from that of Egypt?

Sumer *Egypt*

Map 62: Draw a little bubble sketch of all seven first civilizations, add any rivers, mountains and cities that may be there:

1) 2) 3)

4) 5)

6) 7)

Zooming In 64: After reading the selection, answer the analysis questions that follow:

1)

2)

Quipu

What do the authors mean by 'Norte Chico lighted a cultural fire for many Andean civilizations that followed?

Indus Valley

Irrigation

Note some aspects of the early Indus valley civilization:

Place the four early Chinese dynasties on the timeline below:

2200 b.c. 1800 1500 1000 900 800 700

Son of Heaven

Oracle bones

Oxus valley

What was the Oxus valley civilization the 'focal point' of?

Pic 66: Put a star on the timeline above whereabouts this bronze Shang tiger was made.

Olmecs

Note some of the cultural patterns the Olmecs developed that they passed down to other Mesoamerican cultures:

What were Robert Carneiro's basic arguments?

Uruk

Ziggurat

Epic of Gilgamesh

Mohenjo Daro

Harappa

Pic 70: Characterize the cultural traits of Harappa and Mohenjo Daro in the Indus valley:

Were the institutions of Teotihuacan similar or different than those of the Indus?

Social hierarchy

Code of Hammurabi

Pic 72: Characterize slavery in the following societies:

Mesopotamia *Egypt* *Greek and Roman*

Patriarchy

What kinds of jobs and social roles were available to women in ancient societies?

Jobs *Social roles*

Summarize the ways women were treated differently than men in the following ancient societies:

Mesopotamia	*Assyria*	*Hebrews*	*Egypt*

Ishtar

Hatshepsut

What is your relationship to the state? Is your country governed by the consent of the people, including you, or is it governed by coercion- by force? Before answering, detail how ancient societies were governed:

	Consensual aspects	*Coercive aspects*
Ancient Societies		
My Modern Society		

What propaganda value do you think it gave to Sumerian 'lugals' (rulers) to convince people their symbols of power had divine origin?

Marduk

Pic 77: Estimate the number of students there are in your school:

____

Would it take more or less than five years for all the students in the school working school: together 10/hrs./day to build a ziggurat?

____

Scribe

Snapshot 78: Summarize the chart:

	Type	*Initial Use*	*Example*	*Comment*
Sumer				
Egypt				
Andes				
Indus				
China				
Olmec				

Qin Shihuangdi

Pic 79: Seventeen of these huge heads have been found in Mexico. What was their purpose?

What was the purpose of the temples in Tikal?

Why do you think Herodotus, a Greek visitor to Egypt, known as the 'Father of History' because he wrote some of the first history books and traveled a lot, call Egypt the 'Gift of the Nile'?

This area was more isolated for most of Ancient history: *a. Mesopotamia* *b. Egypt*

Determinism

The *Epic of Gilgamesh* is perhaps the oldest epic story written by human beings. Note some of its themes that centered around big life questions:	How did the Egyptians answer those same questions?

Which society was more pessimistic? *a. Mesopotamia* *b. Egypt*

Map 81: In the cycle of cultures that rose and fell in Mesopotamia, a northwesterly direction up the rivers was the way the capital cities of Sumer, the Akkadian Empire, the Babylonian Empire and the Assyrian Empire went. So, select the correct order of capital cities through time:

a. Ur, Akkad, Babylon, Nineveh *b. Nineveh, Akkad, Babylon, Ur*

The modern capital of Iraq, Baghdad, is located on this, the same river as Nineveh ______________

Historians generalize the reasons societies collapse into 1) environmental changes (either suddenly or over time, as in the case of natural disasters), 2) invasion by outside forces, and 3) terminal social decline, such as an adoption of degenerate morals, the rise of strong class or ethnic conflict, etc. If you were a lawyer arguing all sides of the case, what would your main argument be in defending the following:

Environmental disaster brought down the Sumerian culture	*Invasion brought down Sumerian culture*	*Terminal decline in social values brought down Sumer*

Pharaoh

Day of Judgment

Zooming In 84: After reading the selection, answer the analysis questions that follow:

1)

2)

3)

4)

In AP Psychology, one of the vocab terms is 'superordinate goal.' It is something you want to accomplish, but that you can't do by yourself no matter how hard you try. It is a goal that can only be done with the assembled forces of a group of people. Defending your country against an invading army is an example. Going to the Moon is an example. But there's a catch. It's not easy to get a group of human beings to cooperate in accomplishing a superordinate goal. You have to have some kind of managerial technique, which is one reason historians say the Mesopotamian city-states, and government itself, came into being. Link the *need* for a system of irrigation to exist to support human habitation to 'giant leap' in the quest for order that took place in Mesopotamia:

Pic 86: Most modern Egyptians are descended from Arabs who migrated there after the 7th century A.D., but there has been much controversy surrounding the ethnicity of the *Ancient* Egyptians. Until the 1960s, most historians believed they were Europeans, at least the ruling class, because busts like that of Queen Nefertiti had Caucasian features, and it is well known that Cleopatra, for example, was from a long line of Greek rulers of Egypt. From the 1970s to the 1990s, it was argued by African Studies scholars that the Egyptians were black Africans. Today, the debate still goes on. King Tut's face was reconstructed in 2006 using his mummy, the gold sarcophagus, and DNA evidence, and the result was shown as Caucasian on the cover of National Geographic, adding to the controversy. Yet today's Coptic peoples of Egypt trace their heritage to Ancient times, and their DNA has been linked to haplogroup J from Western Asia. Whether some or many Egyptians were African or not, African mercenaries certainly interacted with the Ancient Egyptians. What are they doing, for example, in Pic 86?

The Bible story of Queen Sheba's visit to the royal court of Solomon in Israel relates that she brought gifts from the Land of Punt on the Red Sea. Where is the Land of Punt in present day terms?

Hittites

Sketch the Nile sideways, with the delta at the left, and label all the way to Meroe, Nubia:

Nice! You went through the Neolithic Transition by settling down to farm and building the first cities. Tired yet?

Pic 104: What does Emperor Qin's tomb of 7,000 terra cotta 'soldiers' tell you about the extent of his political power (taking into consideration this picture, which shows the detail of an individual soldier, all of which had unique features):

Roman scholar Taylor Caldwell first compared modern America to ancient Rome in a 1957 essay called *Honoria.* Her essay centered on what she viewed as the beginning of America's moral decline, and she noted a similar moral decline to decadence having begun before Rome's total collapse.

What is the thesis of the more recent *Are We Rome?*	Do you agree or disagree that America has been in decline for the last few decades or longer?

Note the traits of the political entities we call 'empires,' which are, believe it or not, the most prevalent form of political organization in the last 3,000 years:

Achaemenid ______________________________

Cyrus ______________________________

Ahura-Mazda ______________________________

Darius ______________________________

Satraps ______________________________

According to Herodotus, Persia was *a. a xenophobic* *b. an assimilative* empire.

Map 109: The Royal Road was the superhighway of the Persian Empire. It began in the Kingdom of Lydia, went through Anatolia, Assyria and Babylonia, both Mesopotamian lands, and ended at the capital of Persia, located in Persia proper. Sketch the road below, and label:

Pic 110: From this now-desolate palace, Darius decided to standardized some things to be uniform throughout the while empire, and leave other things to be different depending on what part of the empire you were in. Place an X in the appropriate column for things he standardized and not:

	TAXES	*COINS*	*LANGUAGE*	*RELIGION*
Standardized				
Left to localities				

*For all our talk previously about how much the USA was like Rome, we should add that Persia was kind of like the USA and Rome too, in the sense that like the U.S. and Rome, it had standardized taxes, money and laws. It also had no official language, and neither does the U.S. (not even English though there is a push for it in Congress). Nor was there a state religion in Persia. Also, the Royal Road's postal stations were an ancestor to the U.S. Pony Express, which applied the same strategy when taking mail from Missouri through the Great Plains and Rocky Mountains, to California.

Hellenes

Olympic Games

Map 111: The lie of the land in the interior of Greece, such as where Sparta and Mycenae are, can be best described ast:

a. flat *b. rugged* *c. coastal*

Note the names of six Greek islands:

1) *2)*

3) *4)*

5) *6)*

Athens and Marathon are located in the province of:

a. Macedonia *b. Attica* *c. Laconia*

On the inset map, where did the Greeks *not* colonize?

a. Black Sea coast *b. Southern Gaul*

c. Southern Italy *d. Maghreb, N. Africa*

Citizenship

Greece had a political organization most like *a. Babylonian Empire* *b. Sumerian city-states*

Council of Elders

Helots

Group the following terms that contrast the political, social and economic systems of the two famous polis city-states: *Democracy, Colonization, Austerity, Parthenon, Philosophy, Helots, Militarism, Xenophobia.*

Athens:

Sparta:

Cleisthenes

If monarchy is rule by the one and aristocracy rule by an elite, what is democracy?

Solon came onto the scene in a time of relative crisis for the polis, and made sure his reforms satisfied the aristocrats to a degree, as well as the common people. Revolt by any class would surely have been on his mind. What did Solon and his successors such as Cleisthenes do that placated each class?

FOR ARISTOCRATIC CITIZENS	*FOR COMMON CITIZENS*

The Assembly

Greco-Persian Wars

Ionia

In the 1860s, a Harvard historian named Edward Creasy wrote a book called *The Fifteen Decisive Battles of the World.* The thesis of the book was that if the outcome of any of these battles had gone differently, the world would be a markedly different place now. The first of the fifteen was the Battle of Marathon. Why? If the Persians had won, and Pheidippides (Fuh-dip-eh-dees) would have told his fellow fellow Athenians a different tale, as in, 'uh, we lost,' then the Golden Age of Greece would never have happened. Western Civilization would've been squashed before it began, under Persian foot. It's the ultimate 'alternate 'history' scenario. So, what message *did* Pheidippides deliver before collapsing after running his famous ~26 mile 'Marathon'?

Athens became the strongest polis after the victory over the Persians. They 1) rebuilt the city and 2) formed a coalition called the Delian League. Note the specifics of these two actions:

1) What they built in the city:

2) Characterize the 'imperialism' of Athens:

Peloponnesian War

Philip II of Macedon

Alexander the Great

**Whatever you do, do not Youtube: Iron Maiden Alexander the Great.*

Philip II took advantage of the Greek city-states lack of unity to do what?	What happened to him after his successful effort to conquer and unite Greece?
______________________________	______________________________

Map 115: Alexander the Great led his army across three continents and an amazing 11,000 miles. Note the year in which all the following battles were won by Alexander and his men:

_______ Granicus _______ Issus _______ Gaugamela _______ Hydaspes

Follow Alexander's amazing journey of conquest starting at Pella, Macedonia, and continue to note, in order, the places he conquered and/or visited and-or established, in the manner below:

Land:	*Cities:*	*Land:*	*Cities:*
Macedonia	*Pella*		
Ionia	*Sardis*		
Phoenicia	*Tyre*		
Syria	*Gaza*		
Egypt	*Memphis, Alexandria, Siwa*		

Hellenistic Era ______________________________

Pharisees ______________________________

How did more conservative Jews feel about the trend of Jewish assimilation to Hellenistic Greek culture?

____

Ptolemaic dynasty ______________________________

Pic 116: If the Greco-Persian Wars can be seen as the 'East invading the West,' in Aristotle's terms (he defined Greek civilization as 'Occidental' or 'Western' and Asian civilization as 'Oriental' or 'Eastern'), which direction is the invasion depicted in this image going?

____

Patricians ______________________________

Plebeians ______________________________

Republic ______________________________

'Way of the Ancestors' ______________________________

Latin

Punic Wars

Carthage

The *Forum Romanum* was in a valley between the *Capitoline Hill* (where we get our word 'capitol,' as in capitol of a country, and the *Palatine Hill* (where we get our word 'palace'). It was a meeting place for people to talk about society and politics.

Where do people talk about that these days? Think virtually too!

Rome was an 'aristocratic republic' meaning Patrician males could vote for Senators but Plebeians could not, and law was supreme. Was early America, where only white male property owners over 21 could vote, also an 'aristocratic republic'?

Map 119: The Romans called the Mediterranean *mare nostrum* (our sea)- Why do you think they called it that?

They also named it. *Mediterranean* means 'Middle Earth Sea' in Latin. Can you see why? From the city's perspective, where was it?

Roman names are still used. Whole continents, in fact, got their names from what the Romans called them in the Latin language. For example:

'Africa' was the Roman province on this side of the Mediterranean:

a. North *b. South* *c. East* *d. West*

'Asia,' though not labeled on the map, contained Anatolia, Syria, Arabia and Parthia (Persia). It was to the

a. North *b. South* *c. East* *d. West*

Under Roman law, it was

legal *illegal*

for a man to perform capital punishment on members of his family.

This sound harsh, worse than NFL players using dogs for dogfighting, and going to jail for it despite the dogs being their personal property. Even so, do you think men went around killing their families in Rome? Or do you think that the law allowing and them actually doing are two entirely different things?

Paterfamilias

Pic 120: Resistance to Roman expansion led to the creation of national heroes in Europe. Germans love Arminius (Hermann) who stopped the Romans, Scots and the Irish love Vercingetorix who lost to Julius Caesar in Gaul, and this queen of the Celts, who fought the Romans as well:

During the 1st century B.C., two dominant political parties sprang up in Rome. One called itself the *populares* (Popular party) and styled itself the 'party of the plebeians,' while the other took a more aristocratic turn and appealed to the patricians. It called itself the *Optimates* (Best people's party). Sounds familiar. Can you compare this situation to modern American political parties?

The _______________ *seem like* _______________ *while the* _______________ *seem like* _______________

Octavian Augustus _______________

Pax Romana _______________

Legalism _______________

Han dynasty _______________

Map 123: Note where the Han had influence (any at all) and where it did not:

Korea	*Y*	*N*	*Tibet in the Himalayas*	*Y*	*N*
Vietnam	*Y*	*N*			
Japan	*Y*	*N*	*Taklamakan Desert*	*Y*	*N*

From the perspective of the Chinese, the Silk Road began in the city of _______________

Zooming In 124: After reading the selection, answer the analysis question that follows:

1)

***Tian* (Chinese heaven)** _______________

Mandate of Heaven _______________

While Christianity was introduced to the Romans by the evangelical work of Paul and the early missionaries, Buddhism was introduced to China from India by this group of people:

Who did Buddhism appeal to in China and why do you think a religion promising salvation through nirvana would appeal to these people?

Make a list of some similarities and differences between Roman and Han China:

Similarities *Differences*

Zooming In 128: After reading the selection, answer the analysis questions that follow:

1)

2)

Yellow Turban Rebellion

Xiongnu

Great Wall

The signs of Han decline started in the 100s. To which of the usual suspects did they point?

1) Environmental catastrophe *2) Invasion and conquest* *3) Slow social decline & civil rupture*

The signs of Roman decline started in the 200s. To which of the usual suspects did they point?

1) Environmental catastrophe *2) Invasion and conquest* *3) Slow social decline & civil rupture*

The Year 476

Pic 130: In 452, after the imperial capital had already been sacked by the Visigoths (410), Attila the Hun approached with his warriors. He negotiated not with the emperor, but with the Christian Pope, Leo I. What does that tell you about the power of the emperor in the 5th century?

Note the names of four Germanic 'barbarian' tribes who attacked, settled within, partially assimilated to, but finally brought crashing down the Western Roman Empire:

Aryans

Mauryan dynasty

Arthashastra

Ashoka

Gupta dyansty

What did Faxian, the Buddhist traveler in India, notice about the country?

What did Alaric the Visigothic chieftain demand from Rome?

Map 133: Sketch the map of India at right, labeling the river valleys:

On the map, the rock and pillar edicts point us to the conclusion that this religion was once spread far and wide across India, despite not being very popular there today:

a. Hinduism *b. Buddhism* *c. Jainism*

Now, using this map, add the capital city (Pataliputra):

Pic 134: What was the Great Stupa built for?

When Juvenal cynically used the term Bread and Circuses, he was saying it like this: 'Just give the masses of people food and entertainment, just invite them to the Coliseum and Circus Maximus, just entertain them by tossing rolls of bread up in the stands to them, and you can do whatever you want to them- politically, socially and culturally. The food and entertainment will keep them distracted!' It's something the Soviet KGB or a good propaganda minister would come up with. Yet perhaps we should do some self-analysis. Think of some modern equivalents to the 'Bread and Circuses' concept in our own society. How do Americans you know spend weekends?

Hey! Vizier Ankath just took the papyrus scroll I was trying to read! Gimme back my scroll!

Pic 146: Note the three religious traditions most prevalent historically in China, all depicted in this image:

Age of Warring States

Summarize the 'answers' to the chaos of the Warring States era, presented by the following:

Legalism	*Confucianism*	*Daoism*

Snapshot 151: Summarize the information on the chart related to the following people:

Person	***Date***	***Place***	***System***	***Key Idea***
Zoroaster				
Prophets				
Upanishadists				
Confucius				
Mahavira				
Gautama				
Laozi				
Greek Philosophers				
Jesus				
St. Paul				

Analects

Ren

Filial piety

Pic 152: Modern America's pop culture is largely youth-driven- is that similar or in opposition to the Chinese concept of filial piety?	*Junzi* is the Chinese word for 'superior people.' What characteristics do such people have?

Ban Zhao

What was Ban Zhao's advice in *Lessons for Women?*

Wen

Wu

Laozi

Daodejeing

Pic 155: Daoist symbols like the yin-yang were co-opted in the 1960s by the American hippie movement.

What about this landscape painting gives you a hint as to why the youth of the '60s were interested in Asian systems of philosophy like Buddhism and Daoism?	Draw the Yin-Yang symbol at right:

Hinduism

Vedas

Upanishads

Brahman

Atman

Moksha

Samsara

Karma

In what ways were women relegated to a 'second sex' social role by the Hindu tradition?

Pic 159: Henry David Thoreau, the American author who went into the wilderness outside Boston and stayed in a cabin to write the book *Walden* in the 19th century, believed connection to nature was essential for a full human life. Did the Hindu ascetics agree or disagree with Thoreau?

(Today, perhaps ironically, the suburbs of Boston have overtaken the cabin where he wrote).

Kamasutra

Kali

The Enlightened One

Dukkha

Nirvana

Many belief systems have had a supreme 'goal,' to which adherents strive. In the Greco-Roman belief system dominated by the Olympian gods, the goal was to avoid the underworld of Hades and go to Elysium, a kind of heaven. In the Germanic (Norse) belief, one sought to cross the Rainbow Bridge to Valhalla. In Christianity, salvation come through faith in the existence and power and love of God, his Son, and the Holy Spirit, and achieve Eternal Life in the Heavens above. Summarize the goals of the Buddhist spiritual life, using the terms 'nirvana' and 'extinguished':

Sanskrit

Theravada

Mahayana

Bodhisattvas

Zooming In 162: After reading the selection, answer the analysis questions that follow:

1)

2)

3)

Mahabharata ____________________

Ramayana ____________________

Bhagavad Gita ____________________

Arjuna ____________________

Bhakti ____________________

Vishnu ____________________

Shiva ____________________

Zoroaster (Zarathustra) ____________________

Angra Mainyu ____________________

What was the overarching philosophy of Zoroastrianism?

____

The final decline of Zoroastrianism came with the arrival of this Arabian religion: ________________

Pic 166: What was the purpose of the Fire Altar?

____

Hebrews (Israelites) ____________________

Land of Canaan ____________________

Abraham ____________________

Babylonian exile

Yahweh

Ten Commandments

The Ten Commandments constitute a moral law code often compared with the Code of Hammurabi.

Match the commandment with the ethical idea behind it by drawing a line from one to the other:

1	*Thou shalt have no gods before Me.*	*Respect property rights*
2	*Thou shalt make no graven images.*	*Understand life and death*
3	*Thou shalt not take My name in vain.*	*Guard against jealousy*
4	*Thou shalt keep the Sabbath Day holy.*	*Monotheism*
5	*Honor thy Father and thy Mother.*	*Words have meaning*
6	*Thou shalt not kill.*	*Honor unity in marriage*
7	*Thou shalt not commit adultery.*	*Speak the truth*
8	*Thou shalt not steal.*	*Family, elders and nation*
9	*Thou shalt not bear false witness.*	*More to life than work*
10	*Thou shalt not covet what is thy neighbor's.*	*Careful who and what you idolize!*

'Chosen people'

Note ways the Biblical God differed from the gods of the polytheistic religions surrounding Israel:

Map 167: At right, sketch the map of Ancient Israel. Label the Jordan, the cities, and the seas:

Olympians

Dionysus

Oracle

Rationalism

Socrates

Thales

Hippocrates

Pic 210: Socrates is said to have been poor, without any possessions (he even went around barefoot) except for his toga of course, but his impact is huge- in many ways he started the Great Conversation Western civilization has been having with itself about all the topics in the world for the last 2,500 years... since Socrates.

What was Socrates' method of talking to people?

A democratic jury condemned Socrates to die. What does that say about democracy?

Plato

Summarize what Plato argued in *The Republic:*

Whatever you do, do not Youtube: *Plato's Cave an Allegory in Clay!*

Aristotle

How did Aristotle describe the nature of 'virtue'?

Jesus of Nazareth

Jesus was a Roman subject but not a citizen of the empire. He was born a Jew, living in the Province of:

How was Jesus' background different that that of Gautama the Buddha?

How were Jesus' teachings similar and different to those of the Buddha:

Similar *Different*

St. Paul

Paul was the greatest of the evangelizers of early Christianity. He wrote many letters to different Roman communities (called 'epistles' in the Bible). For example, he wrote about the philosophy of Christianity in his letters to the Corinthians of Greece, the Thessalonians of Thessaloniki (also in Greece), and to the Philippians of the town of Philippi in Thrace, in Greece). He wrote to the peoples of Anatolia too, such as the Ephesians of Ionia (who were Greek), the Colossians in Phrygia (east of Ionia and Lydia in Anatolia), and the Galatian towns of Central Anatolia, east of Phrygia. Finally, Paul wrote a letter to the Romans themselves.

Are you surprised that the New Testament was written in Greek?

What did Paul teach that helped non-Jews embrace Christianity?

New Testament

Christianity spread north and west to Europe by the 300s, eventually being based in Rome. But for the first 200 or so years of its existence, Christianity was centered in the following places:

Jesus spoke a now-extinct language called: *a. Hebrew* *b. Syrian* *c. Aramaic*

The first country to adopt Christianity as a state religion was: *a. Italy* *b. Israel* *c. Armenia*

Map 175: State which belief system, Christianity, Buddhism or Both, diffused to the following regions:

_________________ *Britain* _________________ *China*

_________________ *India* _________________ *Sri Lanka*

_________________ *Spain* _________________ *Armenia*

'Church of the East'

Zooming In 176: After reading the selection, answer the analysis questions that follow:

1)

2)

Before Islam arrived, many Egyptians, Arabs and North Africans were Christian *a. T* *b. F*

Tertullian

Augustine

"The Vandals overran Hippo and burned everything they could not loot. As well, Rome, bastion of order for a thousand years, was buckling, shaking and crumbling before the eyes of all. Pagan barbarianism seemed invincible, and just at this moment, when all else seemed lost and life was at odds with hope, Augustine took up the quill. He wrote to explain to Romans that while the world is in decay and chaos may reign in the City of Man, *the heavens above are alive- the* City of God *is alive. Reform is in the air, but what kind of reform? To Augustine reform meant 'perfecting the individual character' by living and residing in the* City of God, *by reforming the self even if the world collapses around you."*

Adapted from: *Tamm, David, Universal History and the Telos of Human Progress,* 2014

St. Augustine's message in the book *City of God* (426 A.D.) is one of: a. *fear* *b. sadness* *c. hope*

Constantine

Theodosius

The Councils of Nicaea, Chalcedon and Constantinople sought to define an official church position of the following Christian doctrines:

Monophysites

Nestorianism

Historian Norman Davies argues we are observing the decline of what he called *European III,* meaning the modern West is Europe's third incarnation of civilization. *European II* was the Classical civilization of Greece and Rome, which collapsed at the end of the Roman Empire. The Middle Ages that succeeded the empire were what he called *Early European III. European I* was the Minoan-Mycenaean complex that declined first with the destruction of the Minoans when Thera erupted in 1628 B.C., and ended with the collapse of the Mycenaean Greeks after what we call the Trojan War. Remember why societies collapse: 1) environmental catastrophe, 2) invasion and conquest, or 3) terminal social decline (decadence). If Davies is right, then why did *European II* collapse?

First #__________, then #_______

Awesome job! You deserve your own name in hieroglyphics tattooed on this paper, right here →

Pic 190: Why do you think so many artists across most cultures in the world have done sculptures of mothers with their children?

Gandhi supported the idea of class division in India in the 20th century:

a. True *b. False*

How was the Confucian system of merit different than the Indian system?

Meritocracy

Civil service exams

Poem 194: What do you think is the main idea of this poem about success on the big exam?

Bureaucracy

In Classical China, how did one achieve *Mandarin* status, otherwise known as the scholar-gentry?

Scholar-gentry

Wang Mang

Before the year 6, when Wang Mang started his reforms, what was the issue with the land that he wished to tackle?

How did Wang Mang attempt to solve the issue? Was his attempt at 'socialism' successful?

Pic 195: What kinds of jobs are the Chinese peasants doing in this picture?

Zooming In 197: After reading the selection, answer the analysis questions that follow:

1)

'Great Peace'

How were merchants and businessmen (as a group or class) viewed in China?

Casta

Pic 199: Why is this Brahmin paying his workers in this manner?

As one high-caste Indian stated when challenged for being 'mean,' "Imagine sleeping in a room as dirty as a public restroom, where some of the people may have fleas and lice. Now do you see the need for distance?" What do you think about this statement?

a. nasty and judgmental

b. I get his perspective even though it isn't very nice

Varnas

Snapshot 201:

At right, draw a triangle with five levels (called a social hierarchy or caste pyramid) indicating the placement of the castes below, along with a note on the caste's qualities:

Brahmin
Kshatriya
Vaishya
Shudra
Untouchable

Note the stages of life for the Aryan castes:

Stage of Life	*Duties*

Jati

Make a list of some similarities and differences between the Indian and Chinese class systems and their functionality:

Similarities *Differences*

Dharma

Note some ways one could become enslaved in the ancient world:

As opposed to slavery in recent centuries, many slaves in Greece and Rome, who were often of the same ethnic group as their masters, were eventually:

a. freed *b. murdered*

In China, a poor parent might sell their child to a wealthy person, who owned the slave as a:

a. field hand *b. chef* *c. status symbol*

Aristotle believed being held in slavery was good for the slave:

a. T *b. F*

Pic 205: After the Punic Wars were won by Rome, the Legions brought ~55,000 slaves to Italy from many lands, from Greece to Carthage. Spartacus was a Greek slave who led a huge rebellion that was crushed by military force in 73 B.C. But having all this cheap labor around was a double-edged sword. Landowners benefited, but social divisions increased as regular Roman farmers were put out of business by huge farms run by slaves, called latifundia. In fact, the rise of Julius Caesar and the overthrow of the Republic was a direct result of the social anger of regular plebeian Romans. What is the slave doing in this picture?

Latifundia

Note three items produced by the huge commercial farms:

Gladiators

Manumission

Pic 206: Spartacus' slave revolt was defeated in the *north* *boot* of Italy.

Zooming In 208: After reading the selection, answer the analysis questions that follow:

1)

2)

'Patriarchal equilibrium'

Pic 211: Why was feminine inferiority to masculinity so common a belief in China?

Pic 212: What kind of job are these women doing?

During the Tang era in Chinese history, women had a lower status than during the Han era: *T* *F*

Empress Wu

Pic 214: In Greece, as in other societies, women tended to have a more *public* *private* role.

Aspasia

Pericles

What did Spartan women mean when they told their sons, "Come back with your shield, or on it?"

Pic 215: Spartan women's clothes were *more elaborate* *more plain* than Athenian women's.

It is almost a historical irony that Spartan women were freer than both Athenian women *and* Spartan men, in the sense that the men's lives were absolutely militarized and followed a regimen nearly the entire time. How did other Greeks feel about the relative freedom of Spartan women?

The authors write that Spartan women were 'breeding machines' for Sparta's military state. Conversely, however, if men and women never bred offspring, society would go extinct. Do you think the language the authors used is appropriate, or is there more to it than that?

Canoeing to all those islands must have been hard work- almost as hard as reading about it

Pic 228: The most ferocious predatory mammal in Mesoamerica before Columbus' time was the jaguar. There were no lions, tigers, cheetahs, cougars or the like. Bears were here, but only in the north. Why do you think the Mayan rulers liked to associate themselves with the jaguar?

In 1 A.D., historians estimate there were about 250,000,000 people worldwide. Is this more or less than the total population of just the United States today?

In the Andes region, llamas and alpacas were there, but what couldn't they do that other animals in the Eastern Hemisphere could?

Circle all that apply: In which regions of Africa was writing *never* independently developed?

a. North *b. West* *c. Central* *d. East* *e. South*

Snapshot 232: In 2013, the share of the world population living in the United States and Canada amounted to this percentage of the total:

____

____________ is the least populated region

During which year did Africa have the largest share of world population in its history?

____

Which region of the world experienced a massive drop in population between 1500 and 1750?

Why has tropical Africa historically been the most disease-prone continent?

Kingdom of Kush

Meroe

Pic 234: Note some ways that Egypt and Nubia are good examples of cultural diffusion:

Map 235: Axum today is known as the postclassical incarnation of this modern state: ____________

While further north than the modern state, this West African kingdom contained Timbuktu:

Zooming In 236: After reading the selection, answer the analysis questions that follow:

1)

2)

King Ezana

Which church influenced the development of Christianity in the Kingdom of Axum?

a. Roman Catholicism *b. Egyptian Copic* *c. Byzantine Orthodox*

Jenne-jeno

Pic 240: Why do you think this statue represents, as the authors say, a 'resistance to Islam" in West Africa?

The 'highway' or conduit of trade across West Africa was this river:

Unlike the 365-day calendar used in Rome, which was adjusted over time by Julius Caesar, Augustus Caesar and Pope Gregory, and which we use today, Mesoamerican tradition held that there were 260 days in a year. Around this, rituals were based. Is the number of days in a year a matter of opinion from culture to culture, or is there a *correct* number? If so, why?

Mayans

Yucatan Peninsula

Map 242: Note the six famous Mayan cities:

1) *2)* *3)*

4) *5)* *6)*

In which two countries are Mayan cities found in today →

The predecessor culture to the Aztecs in Central Mexico was called: ____________________

Note some of the highlights of the Mayan culture:

Why did historians abandon a romantic view of Mayan culture?

'State shamans'

The signs of Mayan decline started in the 800s. To which of the usual suspects did they point?

1) Environmental catastrophe   2) Invasion and conquest   3) Slow social decline & civil rupture

Teotihuacan

Pyramid of the Sun

Pic 245: If you were a Mayan walking from the Pyramid of the Moon to the Pyramid of the Sun in the distance, what is the name of the road on which you would tread?	Why do you think the street is called that?

What evidence do the authors present to support their contention that Teotihuacan was important long after its collapse of 650?

Chavin

Map 247: Chavin is the most   *northerly*   *southerly*   of the Andean kingdoms.

Who used hallucinogenic plants to get followers to 'see' into the supernatural world?	Do you think they really saw the spirit world?

Moche

How did the El Nino oceanic weather patterns affect Andean cultures?

Summarize the essential cultural attributes of the following:

Wari   *Tiwanaku*

Zooming In 250: After reading the selection, answer the analysis questions that follow:

1)

2)

3)

Aside from being a diffusion of Bantu peoples from West Africa to other parts of the continent, what other living patterns were diffused with them?

Batwa (Pygmy)

The Batwa of Central Africa are the indigenous inhabitants of the Congo Rain Forest. When the Bantu arrived in slow waves, they dominated with their physical height and asserted control over most of the region. The Batwa were marginalized into various pockets of the Congo, where they remain to this day. What do the authors mean when they say regions of Africa were 'Bantuized'?

What is the current status of Bantu-Batwa relations in the Congo? It's a bit dicey. When a British newspaper (*The Independent*, 3/26/2004) investigated, it found strained relations, to the point where the Batwa may become an endangered human group. After a series of guerrilla fighting engagements, the journalists interviewed a Batwa chieftain named Amuzati, taken from his forest home by the Bantu-dominated government, to the capital city of Kinshasa. The journalist reports:

"[Amuzati] loved the city; people outnumbered trees. He fell in with a group of prostitutes he calls his girlfriends. Thanks to the war, deforestation, and visitors like me, the Pygmy's nomadic days are over. It occurs to me that, like everyone else in the forest, Amuzati and his clansmen might want guns to protect themselves. Amuzati looks aghast when I suggest this. 'It would be a big mistake to give us guns- the Bantu would definitely kill us if they thought that we could kill them,' he says... How, I ask Amuzati, did his story reach the world? I go to meet the Catholic Bishop [who broke the story]. 'In the town of Butembo, Bemba's men were cutting fingers and ears off,' he tells me. 'That was normal. But when they started feeding them to the prisoners- that was something new.'"

Why do you think the Bantu have been able to dominate the Batwa for the last 2,000 years?

a. High technology   *b. Physical height and strength*   *c. Better economic system*

The 'age grade' is a term the authors use to describe the rites of passage related to one's age in African kinship-focused cultures. Give an example of a rite of passage an age-grade might embark upon:

In African society | *In American society*

Pic 254: Historians have speculated that the Luba tribe believed women have the ability to hold secret knowledge. How is that belief represented in this sculpture?

Does African animism tend to contain 'once and for all' revelations like the monotheistic religions?

'Gender parallelism'

Anasazi

'Great houses'

Kiva

Pueblo

Map 256: Note the three centers of the Pueblo cultures:

Of the regions of the U.S., circle all that lay in what was at one time inhabited by the Mound Builders:

West Coast *Rocky Mountains* *New England*

Great Plains *Midwest* *South*

Hopewell

Natchez

Describe the social hierarchy of the Natchez tribes:

The Hopewell cultural region had *political unification* *trade relations* with Cahokia.

Oceania

Rapa Nui

Map 259: In the space below, put little dots to indicate the islands of the South Pacific, starting with Easter Island in the east at the extreme right side of this paper, and ending with Palau and New Guinea in the west. Label the islands, and then sketch in the lines for Micronesia, Melanesia, and Polynesia. Include New Zealand but not Australia or 'Island Southeast Asia':

Even small island societies developed significant social hierarchies: *a. True* *b. False*

Tatau

Did women have a different social status than men in the South Pacific? How so?

Note how Mana and Tapu are different:

Pic 261: In *Universal History and the Telos of Human Progress* (2014), the author discussed the historical lesson of Easter Island. Will humanity survive on Earth in the 21st century or will we deplete our resources? Easter Island provides an ominous clue. The people divided up into rival groups, like rival cabins at summer camp, and built the huge *moai* you see in this picture. They used so much of their energy building them, however, that resources became scarce. On the island, there is a high outcropping of rock called Terevaka, a 'Lookout Mountain' from which one can survey *everything*. But that 360-degree full IMAX view did not stop the islanders from cutting the last tree:

"The people who felled the last tree could see it was the last, could know with complete certainty that there would never be another, and they felled it anyway... For a generation or so there was enough old lumber to haul the great stones and keep a few canoes seaworthy for deep water. But the day came when the last good boat was gone. The people then knew there would be little seafood and no way of escape. Wars broke out over ancient planks and worm eaten bits of jetsam. They ate all their dogs and nearly all the nesting birds. The unbearable stillness of the place deepened with animal silences. [Soon] there was nothing left but the moai*, the stone giants who had devoured the land... the biggest [carved face] was 65 ft. long and 200 tons... when Europeans arrived in the 18th century they found one or two living souls per giant statue, a sorry remnant, 'small, lean, timid and miserable.' Their only buildings [were] stone henhouses, where they guarded this last non-human protein from one-another day and night... When Captain Cook returned fifty years later, the people had made war on each other again, and on the* moai *as well; [they were] toppled from their platforms... the ruins littered with human bone. Perhaps it started as the ultimate atrocity between enemy clans, like European nations bombing cathedrals during WWII.'"*

Do you think it is inevitable that our society will collapse like Easter Island eventually, or not?

7 – COMMERCE AND CULTURE

[Silk] Road Trip!!!

Merchant________________

Pic 280: Why do you think camels like this one were the pack animal of choice in the middle of the Silk Road, which linked China with Europe?

How did trade, an economic activity, have the capacity to transform political life?

Answer:

Example:

Silk Road(s)

Silk Road trade is best described as: *a. one long run* *b. a relay race*

The Silk Road prospered most with: *a. strong anchor states* *b. political disorganization*

Map 285. Label the following stops on the Silk Road:

* *

Antioch * * * * * *

Luoyang

* * *

* * Taxila

Snapshot 286: Summarize the products produced for Silk Road trade in each associated region:

China:

Siberia/
Central Asia

India

Middle East

Mediterranean

Silkworms feed on a certain fruit tree, which you probably think is a bush because of the nursery rhyme, but is actually a tree. What is this tree?

How did Chinese women contribute to Silk Road trade?

Note some of the ways silk as a material influence the following cultures:

Roman Empire | *Central Asia* | *Islamic World*

Sogdiana (Sogdia)

Pic 289: Dunhuang became the center of this religion in China ________________________

(On the dot map you did above, find Dunhuang and write the name of this religion next to it in parenthesis)

Summarize how the Silk Road's existence as a transit highway affected world religions:

Summarize how the Silk Road affected diseases:

Note two world religions the Silk Road impacted:

Note two diseases the S.R. impacted:

Sea Road(s)

Why were transportation costs lower on the Sea Road(s) than the Silk Road(s)?

The body of water most associated with the Sea Road(s) before the time of Columbus is:

a. The Atlantic Ocean *b. The Indian Ocean* *c. The Pacific Ocean*

Surat and Calicut were great emporium cities, with warehouses full of Sea Road trade goods. Why were these cities ideally located to be hubs of the Sea Road trade?

Dhows were Arab boats that traded on the western side of the Sea Road, from the East African coat to India. What were junks, and where did they ply the Sea Road trade?

Map 292: In the space below, sketch in the coastline of the Indian Ocean from Sofala, East Africa to Hangzhou, China, the two endpoints of the Sea Road. Label the cities and lands on the route:

Snapshot 294: Summarize the products associated with the following Sea Road regions:

Mediterranean:

East Africa:

Arabia:

India:

Southeast Asia:

China:

Islamic slave trade

The Zanj Rebellion, a slave revolt near Basra in Southern Iraq, which, as the authors state, badly disrupted the Abbasid Empire, lasted this amount of time:

Ali bin Muhammad, who led the revolt, is best compared with:

a. Abe Lincoln b. Spartacus

Srivijaya

Map 296: To the west of the Malay Peninsula lies the ______________________.

Separating Borneo from Java is the ______________________.

Separating Borneo from mainland Southeast Asia is the ______________________ sea.

Separating Celebes and the Moluccas from the Philippines is the ______________________ sea.

Note the major cities of the following kingdoms in Southeast Asia and the Spice Islands:

Pagan *Khmer Empire* *Champa* *Shrivijaya* *Sailendra*

Pic 297: If Borobodur, this temple on the island of Java dates from the 800s, who controlled that island at the time and likely produced it?

Pic 298: If the huge temple complex Angkor Wat was hidden from the mid-1400s to the mid-1800s, when it was found by French missionaries, how long was it taken over by nature and obscured by jungle?

Swahili cities

Map 300: Which Swahili coast city, which had a dual Arab-African culture like all the Swahili cities, lay closest to Great Zimbabwe, the most significant African kingdom in the interior of the continent?

How did Ibn Battuta describe the Swahili cities he visited, such as Kilwa?

Great Zimbabwe

Sand Road(s)

Which desert did the major Sand Road traverse north and south, and east and west?

a. Kalahari *b. Great Salt* *c. Sahara* *d. Gobi*

The Arab term for 'land of black people' is ______________________

Note the kinds of items traded along the Sand Road(s), sometimes called the Trans-Sahara route:

Gold-salt trade

Zooming In 302: After reading the selection, answer the analysis questions that follow:

1)

2)

3)

Map 304: Ghana's kings obtained the gold they traded from the headwaters of the Niger, Senegal and Gambia rivers. This area is

northeast *southwest* of the Kingdom of Ghana.

Mali was *a. larger* *b. smaller* than Ghana.

Mali was *a. larger* *b. smaller* than Spain.

The following city was *not* a destination on the Trans-Sahara trade route:

a. Timbuktu *b. Gao* *c. Niani* *d. Fez* *e. Marrakesh*

'Griot' is the term for the male bards that had a special role in West African society. What was that role?

Ghana

Mali

Slave trading was *a. present* *b. unknown* in West African kingdoms such as Kanem.

Pic 305: Bugs Bunny in the old Loony Tunes cartoons used to send packages (or his antagonists in packages) to Timbuktu, because it is a place so far away, unknown and mysterious. In reality, what was Timbuktu's role in West African life in the Postclassical era?

Zooming In 306: After reading the selection, answer the analysis questions that follow:

1)

Map 308: Did the Aztec merchants called *pochteca* traveled to the Inca capital with products regularly?

Maize (corn) spread from North America to Mesoamerica:

a. True *b. False*

Whatever you do, don't do an image search for 'Heike Crab' – they have samurai faces on their shells!

Pic 322: This Japanese astronomy enthusiast is wearing a Chinese outfit. Why?

Note the four states that historically have 'lived in the orbit of China':

Between the collapse of the Han and the rise of the Sui, China was politically *a. united* *b. fragmented*

Grand Canal ______________________________

Sui dynasty ______________________________

Tang dynasty ______________________________

Song dynasty ______________________________

Hangzhou ______________________________

How did Marco Polo describe Hangzhou?

Map 326: The Grand Canal united these two Chinese rivers?

The Great Wall separated the Chinese from the northern nomads like the Mongolians, but what desert did it also separate China from?

Zooming In 328: After reading the selection, answer the analysis questions that follow:

1)

Pic 330: This image shows us Kaifeng was a: *a. ghost town* *b. bustling marketplace*

Sima Guang ______________________________

Footbinding ______________________________

Pic 332: How did the aristocratic women whose feet were bound get like this- as in- how was it actually done?

'Middle Kingdom'

The Chinese were more like the

a. Greeks *b. Visigoths*

in that they believed themselves to represent civilization while the surrounding peoples were considered 'barbarians.'

Pic 335: How did the tribute system work in practice?

How did the Turkic Uighurs do the Tang a favor?

Uighurs

Khitan

Jurchens

Wang

Silla dynasty

Map 338: Kumsong, which was built based on Korean architects visiting the Chinese capital at Chang'an, was the capital of this Korean kingdom:

Pyongyang, the modern capital of North Korea, considered by the government of the U.S. as a 'rogue state,' was in this postclassical kingdom:

'Free choice' marriage

Hangul

Map 340: During the postclassical era, what is now southern Vietnam was known as:

The city of Hanoi, the modern capital of Vietnam, is on the delta of this river:

Summarize the relationship of Vietnam's aristocracy to China and Chinese culture:

Pic 341: Vietnamese history has been punctuated with influence from China, as we've seen, but also direct political rule. Why is this such a famous battle in the history of Vietnam?

What is *chu nom* and why did it encourage Vietnamese writing to take a new direction?

Shotoku Taishi ______________________________

Nara ______________________________

Heian ______________________________

Today, Heian-kyo is known as ____________________. The city was based on this model:

Like Vietnam and Korea, Japan had cultural influences from China. Summarize them:

Map 342: At right, sketch the four large Japanese islands and label their names, along with the cities:

Pic 343: This person is most equivalent in their class status and function to:

a. A Chinese emperor *b. A European peasant*

c. A European knight *d. An African chief*

Japan fully assimilated its culture to match the Chinese:

a. True *b. False*

Samurai ______________________________

Bushido ______________________________

Kami ______________________________

Zooming In 344: After reading the selection, answer the analysis questions that follow:

1)

Tale of the Genji ______________________________

Murasaki Shikibu ______________________________

Extra: During the Gempei War, two samurai families, the Heiki and Genji, battled it out until the Genji won. The Heike drowned themselves in the Inland Sea, where today, crabs wander with strange markings. Do an image search of *Heike Crab*. Doesn't it look like it has the face of a samurai warrior on it? Weird part: they *only* exist there.

Snapshot 347: Note some important innovations that had their origins in China during the postclassical era:

| Do you think China also adopted technology and innovations from the West? Think of three European or American inventions in use in China:

'Gunpowder revolution'

Fast-ripening rice

How are two seemingly unrelated things, Buddhism and woodblock printing, related?

Until Marxism (communism) was adopted in China in 1949, there was only major 'cultural borrowing' (as opposed to a technological or scientific borrowing) that radically affected Chinese civilization.

What was it? Where did it come from? How did it get to China?

Note the role of the Buddhist monasteries in China during the postclassical era:

| The Buddha dharma (rule code) was translated into Chinese as *dao* (the way). Why do you think the translators picked this specific word?

Sui Wendi

How, in specific terms, did the Sui:

Use Buddhism to justify their wars *Reward Buddhism with patronage*

Map 350: Isn't it strange that Tibet remained 'purple' for so long? Thinking in terms of physical geography and trade routes, why might this isolated Himalayan region not receive the teachings of the Buddha until after they had been diffused all across the rest of East and Southeast Asia?

An Lushan Rebellion

After the An Lushan Rebellion, Han Yu and other Confucian scholars:

a. gave in to Buddhist diffusion *b. criticized Buddhism as a foreign cultural invasion*

9 – THE WORLDS OF ISLAM

Mecca is the Islamic Mecca

Caliph ______________

Pic 362: Where are these Muslim pilgrims going? | Why?

As a percentage of the world's population today, about how many are Muslims? ______________

Bedouins

Blood feud

Mecca

Kaaba

Quraysh

Members of these two older religions lived among the Arabs on the Arabian Peninsula:

| Allah was supreme god of the Arab pantheon, like Jupiter was supreme in the Roman pantheon. What did Allah become over time?

Map 366: The two large empires that bound the Arabian Peninsula on the north were the:

1)

2)

| When Muhammad fled Mecca to Medina, the *Hijra,* which direction did he travel?

a. North *b. South*

c. East *d. West*

Muhammad ibn Abdullah

Khadija

Quran

Pic 367: In this image, Muhammad is leading prayers with the following religious figures from other traditions in audience:

1)

2)

3)

| The creators of *South Park* were under threat of death because they were going to portray Muhammad's face on their cartoon. Muslims believe it is a sacrilege to show his face. Do they show it in your textbook?

The other major AP World textbook, *Traditions & Encounters 6th edition,* says, "Allah was the same omnipotent, omniscient, omnipresent and exclusive deity as the Jews' Yahweh and the Christians' God" (pg. 293 if your teacher has it by chance and you want to verify this). What does the Strayer textbook say about the relationship of Allah to the Jewish and Christian God(s)?

Your turn to take a position. Being that the Jewish God in the Torah and Talmud has a different set of expectations for those he calls his 'Chosen People,' and the New Christian God of the Bible is in essence a trinity of Father, Son, and Holy Spirit, a concept not considered in Judaism or in the Islamic notion of Allah, who outlines another different set of expectations for people in the Quran, to what extent to you agree these Gods, or these concepts of God, are really talking about the same deity? If you were a lawyer arguing first for one side and then for the other, as- recall- good debaters practice doing- what would your main points be?

They are the same God	They are different gods

'Seal of the prophets'

Muslim

Umma

List the Five Pillars of Islam and the meaning of each:

	Pillar	*Meaning*
1)		
2)		
3)		
4)		
5)		

Hajj

Jihad

How are *Greater Jihad* and *Lesser Jihad* different?

Muhammad's message was *a. welcomed* *b. rejected* by the Meccan community.

Hijra

How much of Arabia had Muhammad's forces converted to Islam by the end of his life?

a. not much *b. about half* *c. most*

Regarding marriage, Muhammad encouraged Muslims to:

a. be monogamous like European Christians

b. be polygamous like African animists

How did the birth of Islam differ from the birth of Christianity?

Recently, Muslims living in Great Britain have successfully lobbied for a separate sharia court system for themselves, something Akbar may have endorsed. Both litigants must agree to have their legal matter settled by either the *Muslim Arbitration Tribunal* or the *Islamic Sharia Council.* If one does not, the case goes to the regular British court. Do you agree with the idea that different ethnic or religious groups in a country should have their own self-determined rules and laws, or should everyone in a country be subject to the same rules and laws? If you were a lawyer arguing both sides of the case, what would your main points be?

Muslims (and others) should have different rules	Everyone should have the same rules

Sharia

Arab armies invaded and destroyed the Persian (Sasanian)Empire in 644. How long did it take them to do that from the time Muhammad died in 632?

Muslims viewed their religion as an ethnic religion for Arabs only:

a. True *b. False*

Battle of Talas River

Dhimmis

Jizya

Map 372: Which lands (caps) and cities (lower case) did Islamic armies take during these times:

LANDS *CITIES*

Before 632:

632-656:

656-750:

750-900:

Use the map to find out who was on the other side of each directional border of the *dar al-Islam* as of 800:

NORTHWESTERN (IN EUROPE):

SOUTHEASTERN (IN ASIA):

NORTHEARSTERN (IN ASIA):

SOUTHERN (IN AFRICA):

EASTERN (IN ASIA):

NORTHERN (PAST SYRIA):

Shahnama

Caliph

Rightly Guided Caliphs

Abu Bakr

Sunni

Imam

Ali

Shia

Sunni-Shia schism

Pic 376: What is the actual central part of the ritual during the Hajj that should be accomplished?

Umayyad dynasty

Ulama

Pic 377: What was the role of the *sufi* in Islamic society?

Zooming In 378: After reading the selection, answer the analysis questions that follow:

1)

2)

Al-Ghazali

In Christian churches, men and women sit together.

What did Umar legislate in this dynamic? | What did Mansur legislate regarding this?

Umar

Mansur

'Honor killing'

Clitoridectomy (yikes)

Hadiths

Mullah

Abbasid dynasty

While the Umayyad dynasty used Damascus in Syria as their capital city, where did the Abbasids move the capital of the caliphate?

Map 383: This other city rose during the Abbasid dynasty's rule of the caliphate. It is on this map in northern Egypt:

Map 383: List all the lands Ibn Battuta traveled to:

Sultanate of Delhi

Bhakti

Guru Kabir

Guru Nanak

Sikhism

Map 384: The Sultanate of Delhi, the first instance in which a Muslim elite ruled a generally Hindu population, controlled the lands of Northern India. Pradesh, in the middle of the Ganges basin, is not on the map. But three lands are. Name the three:

| The west coast of India, a center for
| trade on the Indian Ocean route, is
| called the
| ________________ coast.
|
| The east coast is called this:
|
|

Ottomans

The Ottomans defeated the Christian Byzantine Empire in 1453 by taking Constantinople. Then they expanded into Europe, absorbing the lands of (circle all that apply):

a. Italy *b. Greece* *c. Bulgaria* *d. Russia* *e. Wallachia (Romania)*

In the areas ruled by the Muslims, Christians were often not allowed to hold church services: *T* *F*

Map 387: Islam diffused to West Africa on this route:

a. Silk Road *b. Sand Road* *c. Sea Road*

| Among the larger African kingdoms,
| only this one resisted Islamic inroads:
|
|

Pic 388: What historical process does this building represent?

| Islam took hold in West Africa
|
| *a. everywhere* *b. among the elites*
|

Sonni Ali

Christians in Spain during the time Muslims ruled it as *Al-Andalus,* were given greater or lesser freedom depending mostly on:

a. the whims of the rulers *b. their ability to learn Arabic*

When did the era of Islamic rule over Spain end?

| Which Spanish king and queen completed the
| Christian *Reconquista* of Spain?
|
|

Cordoba

Granada

After the Christian Spaniards took over in Spain, what policies did they effect toward the following:

Muslims *Jews*

Zooming In 390: After reading the selection, answer the analysis questions that follow:

1)

2)

Madrassas

Shaykhs

'Islamic Green Revolution'

Snapshot 395: Summarize the information on the chart related to the following people:

Person	***Contribution***
Al-Khwarazim	
Al-Razi	
Al-Biruni	
Ibn Sina	
Omar Khayyam	
Ibn Rushd	
Nasir al-Din	
Ibn Khaldun	

If you get any wrong, see you in Saturday School detention. If you get everything right, see you in Valhalla. Up to you.

Pic 408: How do you know Charlemagne was a Christian monarch?

In the story of Yao Hong from modern China, why do you think Christianity is growing there while it declines in our own society?

While Christianity existed in North Africa when it was still a series of Roman provinces, and in the Middle East, following the Islamic conquests, Christianity was primarily the religion of this continent:

While the southeastern side of Europe was Orthodox, the western side of Europe was primarily this in the Middle Ages:

If one dug into the foundations of the Islamic mosque of Sana'a in Yemen, one would find this:

Pic 412: This site in Jerusalem is a 'sacred space' for three religious faiths. What does it represent for each?

Jews *Christians* *Muslims*

When the Islamic caliphate conquered Christian territory such as Palestine and North Africa, conversion was effected:

a. by the sword *b. through voluntary means* *c. both*

Pic 413: This stele is proof that Yao Hong's story is: *a. an old one* *b. something totally new*

How did the Jesus Sutras describe Christianity to the Chinese?

In Egypt, when was Christianity replaced by Islam as the majority religion?

In Nubia when was Christianity replaced as the majority religion?

Pic 415: In the lone Christian kingdom in Africa, ____________________, churches were built differently than in Europe, where their spires reached for the sky. How were they built in Ethiopia?

Constantinople

Justinian

Map 417: This map is from the time after the Fall of Rome but before the Islamic takeover. In that 150-year period, the Byzantines tried to rebuild the whole Roman Empire and bring it back. Circle the places where they were successful, at least temporarily:

Northern Spain *Southern Spain* *France* *North Africa* *Italy* *Britain*

While in Western Europe the pope was a religious figure and a king was a political figure, in the Byzantine world, what was the relationship between church and state?

Caesaropapism

Like modern sports fans that form gangs after soccer matches in Europe and other places, the Greens and the Blues were antagonistic gangs in the Byzantine Empire. What sport were they crazy about?

Note the ways in which the following considered the nature of Christ and God:

Arius (Arianism) *Holy Trinity*

Icons

Iconoclasm is the belief that images like pictures of Jesus and Mary, or of saints, are sacrilegious.

Which side of Europe, the Catholic or Byzantine side, temporarily banned icons?	Would you consider Muslims iconoclasts?

Pic 420: Byzantine churches like St. Mark's in Venice featured both arches and domes: *T* *F*

Greek Fire

Bezant

Byzantine Orthodox influences were diffused to this group of people in Europe:

a. Germanic Northern Europeans *b. Slavic Eastern Europeans*

Cyrillic alphabet

Zooming In 422: After reading the selection, answer the analysis questions that follow:

1)

2)

Kievan Rus

Perun

The Viking explorers ranged far and wide. Sometimes they raided churches in Ireland, other times they sailed up the River Seine to Paris and freaked out the locals. They colonized Iceland, and ventured, by all accounts in their sagas, to America for a brief moment. They also went the other way, and showed up in Kievan Rus, where Rurik became the first king of the Russians. Why do you think the 12 Rus tribes selected a foreigner, someone who was not of them, to be their first king?

Some peoples in history have ascribed a certain 'specialness' to themselves that supersedes their existence as simply an identifiable people with a unique culture. The Jewish Israelites have considered themselves a 'chosen people' for perhaps three thousand years. Roman Christians considered themselves the perfection of the Biblical prophecies, having been redeemed by Jesus' sacrifice on the Holy Cross. But the Roman Empire collapsed, and with it, the 'power center' of the faith, which moved to Constantinople. With the collapse of Constantinople to the Turks in 1453, however, that torch was passed on to the Russians, who came to see themselves as a people set apart, and Moscow became the 'Third Rome.' What empire was Constantinople the capital of before it fell and passed the torch to Moscow?

Vladimir I

'Russification'

Historians used to call the Early Middle Ages the Dark Ages, from about 500-800. The idea was that the 'light of civilization' was almost extinguished. Art historian Kenneth Clark, in the most famous history documentary ever, said of this era, "We got through by the skin of our teeth." What happened to the roads and buildings of the empire during this time?

The Germanic kingdoms of the Middle Ages

a. assimilated *b. rejected all aspects of*

Roman law.

Summarize the value the Gothic leader Athaulf saw in Roman state structures:

Woden (Odin)

After the migrations of Late Antiquity, known in German as the *volkerwanderung,* the following Germanic peoples found homes in semi-permanent places of settlement:

The Germanic peoples tended to live in kinship-based tribes with

a. strong *b. weak*

warrior values.

Charlemagne

Christmas Day, 800

Otto I

Holy Roman Empire

Map 426: Charlemagne's empire split into _______ sections after his death, which became the basis for the future separation of France from Germany and Northern Italy.

Feudalism

In the lord-vassal relationship of Medieval Europe, sometimes known as the 'feudal contract,' what did each offer the other?

The lord offered the vassal: *The vassal offered the lord:*

Serfs

In the USA, territory is overseen by three levels of government: federal, state and local. At the federal level, the whole land is overseen by a president, but subdivided into states overseen more closely by governors, while states are subdivided into even smaller units like cities and counties, overseen by commissioners and mayors. During Roman times, the emperor oversaw the entire territory, but subdivided it to provincial and city leaders as well. But those subdivisions are political. In Medieval Europe, the pope was like the president, who oversaw all of Christendom, and who subdivided it to be overseen by cardinals, archbishops, bishops and parish priests. In this sense, the parish priest is most like:

a. A president *b. A governor* *c. a mayor* *d. a missionary*

Global warming is a modern phenomenon and did not happen in the Middle Ages *a. T* *b. F*

Map 429: Physically, the largest European kingdom was:

a. The Holy Roman Empire of the German Nation *b. Poland* *c. Kievan Rus*

Follow the arrows and note the places within Christendom which were assaulted by the following:

1) Vikings:

2) Muslims:

3) Magyars:

Of the three above, which are the people known today as *Hungarians*? ____________________

Make a bar graph illustrating the populations of the following cities in the Middle Ages:

1,000,000

750,000

500,000

250,000

100,000

50,000

1

Hangzhou *Cordoba* *Constantinople* *Venice* *Paris* *London*

Guild

A Medieval guild of workers in Europe was most equivalent to:

a. the jati subcastes of India *b. the scholar-gentry of China* *c. the samurai of Japan*

What kinds of jobs did women hold in European places during the Middle Ages?

Zooming In 432: After reading the selection, answer the analysis questions that follow:

1)

2)

Hildegard of Bingen

Anchoress

Map 435: If during the first half of the Middle Ages (500-1000), Europe was assailed by attackers such as the Muslim armies which assaulted Spain, France, Southern Italy and the Byzantine territories, during the second half of the Medieval era (1000-1500), it was Europeans who pushed out in every direction. Match the arena of action with the appropriate direction the expansion moved:

Reconquista against Muslims in Spain	_______	*a. Northwest*
Crusading against Muslims in Jerusalem	_______	*b. Southwest*
Spreading the Gospel to the Prussians	_______	*c. Northeast*
Colonizing Iceland, Greenland, Vinland	_______	*d. Southeast*

This crusade was directed against the Prussian pagans of Northern Poland and Russia: ___________

Summarize the situation in each Crusade and state whether the crusaders used a sea route or not:

1st Crusade

2nd Crusade

3rd Crusade

4th Crusade

1099

Crusader

How did the Crusades help inspire a greater amount of trade from Asia and the Middle East to Europe?

Pic 436: The Europeans who went on Crusades

a. assimilated to Islamic culture

b. built European-style kingdoms

Godefroi de Bouillon

Bernard of Clairvaux

Pic 440: When it says God was seen by Europeans as a divine engineer, what did that mean?

Name three kinds of complex gearing mechanisms invented by High Medieval Europeans:

1) *2)* *3)*

Quote 441: What three future inventions used by us did Roger Bacon predict 800 years ago:

1) *2)* *3)*

Banks appeared in Italian cities like Genoa and Venice (Ever heard of Shakespeare's play *The Merchant of Venice*? Now is a good time to act it out as a class project. Go ahead: *Youtube* it, and see if your teacher will let you do that instead of taking the next test. Seriously, ask. We'll wait). What kinds of services do banks offer that help spur business and investment?

List the Three Estates and their attributes:

1)

2)

3)

Aquinas and Bacon reasoned that God *wanted* his people on earth to study the grand designs of created nature. This meant studying about the universe and everything that constitutes it. The goal of scholasticism was to please the Christian God by learning more and more. Is it a surprise that the first universities, Bologna, Paris, Oxford and Cambridge, appeared at this time, and that Europe stood poised on the brink of a scientific revolution? Why or why not?

'Natural philosophy'

Pic 444: The oldest university in the world is the University of Bologna, Italy. This is an image of students in class. What is similar and what is different between these students and your class?

Similar *Different*

Imagine trading places in time with one of your Medieval ancestors. What kind of job or lifestyle do you think you would have in the Middle Ages?

---

11 – PASTORAL PEOPLES ON THE GLOBAL STAGE

They're the exception… nomad-der what

Khan_______________

Pic 456: Does this painting give us any clues about why the Mongolian peoples were so mobile- able to travel great distances and live off the land?

Some of the resources provided by animals to pastoral societies were:

Kinship groups

Snapshot 460: Summarize the primary animals and features of the following nomadic peoples:

	Location/Region	*Animals*	*Features*
Xiongnu, Yuezhi, Turks, Uighurs, Mongols, Huns			
Seljuks, Ghaznavids Il-khans, Uzbeks, Ottoman Turks			
Arab Bedouins, Berbers, Turareg			
Fulbe, Nuer Turkana, Masai			
Sami Nenets			
Tibetans			
Inca			

Pic 461: The Scythians were a pastoral people during Roman times. What evidence is there on this necklace of that lifestyle?

'Fictive kinship'

Manichaeism

Modun

Map 463: These days, national borders are generally well defined on maps and in reality. In the past, the border areas between states or cultures were often ill-defined. In fact, people would speak of 'frontiers' instead of fixed 'borders.' The country Ukraine, for example, between Russia and Poland, actually means 'frontier' in Slavonic languages because it tended to be an area historically separating the two powers. What evidence to you see on this map that demonstrates the idea that between the Han realm and the Xiongnu Confederacy was a 'frontier' and not a fixed 'border'?

Of the following pastoral peoples, the Seljuks were a dynasty from this group:

a. Arabs *b. Turks* *c. Mongols* *d. Xiongnu* *e. Berbers*

Kaghan

Note two ways the Turkic peoples of Central Asia influence Chinese culture:

1) *2)*

Why did Turkic leaders begin calling themselves *sultan* instead of *kaghan* by the 12th century?

Ibn Yasin

Map 465: The Almoravid Empire's religion was ________________ and its capital was __________

These two Spanish cities were never part of the Almoravid Empire:

a. Cordoba and Seville *b. Toledo and Valencia* *c. Tangier and Fez*

Contrast how the Mongol cultural 'footprint' in the region they ruled differed from the Arab imprint which still exists strongly in the Middle East and North Africa:

Mongol-style *Arab-style*

Temujin

Map 466: *Sarai was the capital of this Mongol domain:* ______________________

Baghdad was the capital of this Mongol domain: ______________________

Samarkand was the capital of this Mongol domain: ______________________

Khanbalik (Beijing) was the capital of this Mongol domain: ________________

What should we call the Mongol chieftain who conquered this vast realm in green? A century ago, historians like H.G. Wells (who wrote *War of the Worlds*) spelt his name Jenghis Khan. Then in the 1960s, books started spelling his name Genghis because English-speakers said it like that. Then in the 2000s, it was decided by some writers to de-Anglicize his name, in an attempt to reflect the sound one is to make while saying it in Mongolian. So it became 'Chinggis.' Make a trill sound: 'Cing!' Like a cash register, then a 'hiss.' If you were a lawyer arguing both sides, what would your main points be in persuading people to:

Keep the English-friendly spellings	Change spellings to reflect local pronunciations

What year did the 'Mongol world war' begin? ______________________

Modern scholars estimate that the Mongols killed over 16,000,000 people during their conquest of Asia and Eastern Europe. Being that the Mongol nation as a while numbered around 1,000,000, about how many people were killed for every Mongol alive?	Pic 469: How many people were there in China for every Mongol like the one shown here?

Zooming In 470: After reading the selection, answer the analysis questions that follow:

1)

Karakorum ______________________

The Mongols, like the Muslims, demanded conversion to their religion: *a. T* *b. F*

Ogodei Khan ______________________

Yuan dynasty ______________________

Khanbalik ______________________

Pic 474: Marco Polo visited Xanadu Palace, built by this khan: *a. Chingghis* *b. Batu* *c. Khubilai*

Chabi

Il-khan Hulegu

What happened to the Abbasid capital of Baghdad?

Il-khan Ghazan

Rashid al-Din

Zooming In 477: After reading the selection, answer the analysis questions that follow:

1)

Pic 478: The authors perhaps provocatively titled this caption, "Mongol Rulers and Their Women." Why do you think they used those terms to describe this image?

Kipchak

Pic 479: After Polish rulers refused to submit to Batu Khan, the Mongols assaulted Krakow, Poland's Medieval capital city. As the Mongol force appeared by night, the lookout man in in the spire of St. Mary's church saw the approach. He took out his trumpet and played a song to wake up the population of the town. In the middle of the song, a Mongol arrow from beyond the city wall pieced his throat, and he collapsed, dead. To this day, every hour the 'wake up song' is played by a trumpeter in the same church spire. People in the cafes below on the city square listen on- a reminder of the Mongol invasion from so long ago. (Youtube: *Hejnal Mariacki* to hear the song, and notice how it cuts off right in the middle of a note). After this battle, a coalition of German and other European knights held back the Mongols at the Battle of Liegnitz, while two decades later in 1260, the Egyptian Mamelukes defeated them at Ain Jalut. Not long after the scene pictured here, Baghdad surrendered. What did Hulegu order his troops to do to the people inside the city?

Khan Guyuk

Black Death

Map 482: In which body of water is the peninsula that Caffa, the city where the Mongols may have committed what we now call bioterrorism, located?

Map 482: The likely source of the Bubonic Plague of the 13th century was:

a. Egypt *b. India* *c. Western China* *d. Italy*

The last places in Europe to get the plague were: *a. Italy & Britain* *b. Scandinavia & The Baltics*

The authors state this is one of the most important maps in the book. That being the case, draw not the land masses, but *only* the trade route circles, starting with the biggest one, and label the cities on them:

List the symptoms of the Black Death:

About how many of Europe's people died of the plague during the 14th century, according to recent studies?

Pic 485: The Bubonic Plague has totally eradicated from the face of the earth forever: *T* *F*

One side-effect of the plague was the stalling of trade along the Silk Road. Imagine now that the U.S. highway system that connects cities many hundreds of miles apart all of a sudden was blocked off and trucks could not get through. Think of five products at the grocery store that you would not have access to anymore:

---

 12 – THE WORLDS OF THE 15TH CENTURY **Explorer**______________

Time to make a mental Munster map of everything in this chapter. Look it up.

Pic 498: Do you think the artist who painted this picture of Columbus agreed with Winona LaDuke or with the Americans of 1892 who celebrated him as a heroic figure? Why?

List regions of the world that were still Paleolithic-type societies in the 1400s:

How was hunter-gather (Paleolithic) life different in the Americas than in Australia? Note some characteristics:

Australia *Americas*

Igbo

'Stateless society'

Songhay

Pic 503: *Genomebiology.com* reports that a large 2009 study found most black Americans came from the Yoruba and Mande tribal affiliations. Both the Yoruba and Mande live today near where this mask was made in the postclassical era, in and around what are now Nigeria, Ghana (the former Songhay Empire) and Benin. These places are all located in:

a. Southern Africa *b. Central Africa* *c. West Africa* *d. East Africa*

Note the names of the *Five Nations* of Iroquois-speaking peoples:

Great Law of Peace

Timur

Fulbe

Islam was diffused to the Fulbe of West Africa by jihads in these centuries: ______________

Ming dynasty

Yongle

Yongle's Encyclopedia

Forbidden City

Map 506: Tamerlane's empire, though short-lived, included all but the following:

a. Samarkand, Central Asia *b. Isfahan, Persia* *c. Delhi, India*

Eunuch

Zheng He

List five exotic products brought back to China from the voyages of Zheng He:

Pic 507: If you were a eunuch at the Ming court and a traveler from Europe appeared, like Marco Polo a century before, how would you explain the meaning of this building?

Map 506: Imagine being on Zheng He's voyage of exploration in the South Pacific and Indian Ocean. Follow your route out from Changzhou and list the places you went in order, ending at Mombasa on the Swahili Coast:

Zooming In 508: After reading the selection, answer the analysis questions that follow:

1)

2)

3)

What rationale did the Ming rulers have for 'grounding' Zheng He's fleet?

"The 15th century admiral Zheng He, who sailed the Indian Ocean blue in huge treasure ships, was grounded by his Ming overlords. Had he not been, historians speculate China could have discovered and colonized America's west coast, could have dictated terms of trade to the Europeans (and everyone else), and could have done many other things. But it chose not to, it chose to end the exploration project, in large part, by nothing more than the diktat of its leaders, who were interested in domestic politics. Because these leaders chose to look inward, the world's largest nation did not contribute to the Age of Exploration. This is a mighty lesson for us, as today the leading exploring nation of the 20th century, the United States, is doing the same thing. By the diktat of its leaders, such as the Congressional Budget Committee, the United States has grounded its space exploration fleet and its astronauts, just like Zheng He. Just as his treasure ships were scuttled half a millennium ago, so have U.S. orbital shuttles, moon-ships, and interplanetary spacecraft been scuttled today. Like Ming China, the USA now looks inward, only with no more frontier to explore, and without considering the seemingly insoluble social problems it now faces, may in fact be exacerbated by this very inward focus." –David Tamm, Universal History, 2014

What is the author's point-of-view in the above passage?

Do you agree or disagree?

Contrast China's political organization was that of a unified empire under the Ming. How was Europe's political configuration different?

Hundred Years' War

To Europeans of the Renaissance era, Christianity was:

a. one religion of many *b. the one true religion, and all others are false*

Map 514: All the major kingdoms in Africa in the 15th century were centered on the banks of rivers. Match the river with the appropriate kingdom or empire:

Congo *Niger-Senegal* *Nile* *Zambezi*

Ethiopia *Kongo* *Songhay* *Zimbabwe*

Ottomans

The Ottoman rulers claimed they were the inheritors of all of the following except:

a. the Persian Empire *b. the Abbasid Caliphate* *c. the Prophet's succession*

Safavids

The Ottoman, Safavid and Mughal Empires were similar in that:

a. They had a Persian ruling class *b. They had a Turkic ruling class* *c. They had an Indian ruling class*

The Safavids were Shia Muslims, meaning they:

a. Favored Abu Bakr as Muhammad's successor *b. Favored Ali as Muhammad's successor*

Map 517: This is going to be an exercise in ID'ing bodies of water without them being labeled on this map. Select which of the three Islamic Gunpowder Empires fits the criteria best:

a. Ottoman Turkey *b. Safavid Persia* *c. Mughal India:*

_____ dominates coastlines _____ Caspian & Persian Gulf _____ borders both others

_____ includes the Ganges River _____ includes Islam's holy city _____ expanded in Europe

Zooming In 518: After reading the selection, answer the analysis questions that follow:

1)

2)

Sonni Ali

Mansa Musa was the only West African ruler to make an elaborate hajj to Mecca: *a. T* *b. F*

Janissaries

Pic 520: 'Ethos' is a Greek word that means the defining characteristic, or spirit, of a culture or group of people. So, usually, the 'ethos' of a corporation is to sell goods and services and make money. What was the ethos of the Janissary slave warriors?

Mughal Empire

The most difficult cultural issue the Mughals faced in their rule over India was being a

a. Christian *b. Jewish* *c. Muslim* *d. Buddhist*

minority faced with ruling over a vast Hindu majority.

Why was the early modern era discussed here seen as a 'second flowering of Islam'?

Malacca

Despite being on total opposites sides of the Eastern Hemisphere, what did Malacca and Timbuktu share during this era?

____

Mexica ____

Lake Texcoco ____

Tenochtitlan ____

Map 523: This city was built by the Mayans: *a. Tenochtitlan* *b. Cuzco* *c. Chichen Itza*

Geographically, the Iroquois Confederation was in this section of the modern United States:

a. West Coast *b. Great Plains* *c. Northeast* *d. South*

What was the primary activity of Caribbean islanders? ____

____

Pochteca ____

The Aztecs had a strict schedule of human sacrifice. Bernardino de Sahagun was a Spanish ethnographer who was fascinated by the possibility of studying the Aztec culture. He went to Mexico and spent 50 years studying everything he could about them. His *Florentine Codex* is the most detailed analysis in existence of pre-Columbian America. He was disturbed, like many Spanish, by Aztec religion. From the *Florentine Codex:*

MONTH	WHO AND HOW
February	*children and captives to water deities*
Early March	*captives and gladiators, priest wore skin of flayed victims while dancing*
Late March	*hearts cut out, ritual burying of skin, children sacrificed*
April	*maidens, teenagers*
Early May	*focus is on hearts being cut out of commoners*
Late May	*focus on drowning commoners*
June	*decapitation of women*
July	*starvation in cave or temple*
Early August	*burning*
Late August	*decapitate woman, man wears her skin, people thrown off pyramid*
September	*cut out heart, burn*
Early October	*children, noblewomen cannibalized*
Late October	*bludgeoning, decapitation*
Early November	*large-scale sacrifices of slaves and captives*
Late November	*children and slaves decapitated*
Early December	*heart cut out and body decapitated*
Late December	*Night sacrifices by fire*
January	*Festival days of fasting, no sacrifices*
Late December	Night sacrifices by fire

What was the rationale Aztec society had for undertaking so many human sacrifices?

What was the purpose of the 'floating gardens' *(chinampas)* made by the Aztecs around their capital city?

Pic 524: What are some of the jobs Aztec women had?

Tlacaelel ____

Huitzilopochtli ____

Inca Empire ____

Quechua ____

Inti ____

Quipu ____

Cuzco ____

Pic 527: While Cuzco was the Inca culture center, it is the amazing mountaintop city of Machu Picchu that is always shown as a postcard image of the culture. It was unknown to the Spanish when Pizarro conquered the Incas in 1533, and remained undiscovered until 1911. How many years is that?

Describe the *Mita* labor system that the Inca used (and that the Spanish would later employ as well):

'Gender parallelism' ____

Sapay ____

Coya ____

Map 530: The city that sat on the very border of the Christian and Muslim words in 1450:

The largest of the major religions in *land area*:

The city in southern Spain that remained Muslim longer than the rest of Spain:

The religion of the Swahili (East African) coast:

Snapshot 532: After which century's turn did the world population reach a billion? ____________

Teacher: "You got an F on the last test." Student: "Yeah, well, it's because I copied over the shoulders of midgets."

Pic 552: Shah Jahan, pictured here, famous for building the Taj Mahal for his deceased wife as a tomb, was a Turkic and Muslim imperialist governing India, a land that was neither Turkic nor majority Muslim. While 'imperialist' wasn't considered an insult to Shah Jahan, why do you think it is used as a slur today?

This European country did not engage in overseas imperialism outside Europe during the Colonial Era:

a. Britain *b. France* *c. Germany* *d. Spain* *e. Portugal*

Recalling that the Silk Road trade was a relay with many exchanges of product for currency, and recalling the bad blood between Christian Europe and the Islamic Middle East, why do you think the Europeans wanted to 'go around' the Muslims to trade directly with India and the Spice Islands?

Map 556: Note the correct imperial rules of the following lists of cities:

Rio de Janeiro	*Lima*	*Jamestown*	*Quebec*
Sao Paolo	*St. Augustine*	*Boston*	*New Orleans*
____________	____________	____________	____________

Hernan Cortes

When Cortes arrived to Mexico with a crew of conquistadors from Spain, why did some Native American groups like the Tlaxcalans ally with them against the Aztecs?

Who was involved in the Inca family dispute that helped Pizarro and the Spanish?

Germs

Zooming In 558: After reading the selection, answer the analysis questions that follow:

1)

2)

Name some diseases the Native Americans had little or no exposure or immunity to:

New Netherland

The Great Dying

Little Ice Age

Climate change, called today 'global warming' in popular culture because the average temperature of the world is said to be rising instead of falling, is a fact of life. In the 16th century, people would have thought of climate change as:

a. global warming *b. global cooling*

How did the 'General Crisis' affect the following places:

Northern lattitudes *Equatorial regions* *Europe* *China* *Mexico*

Columbian exchange

Summarize the major effects the Columbian Exchange had on the New World and Old World:

Diseases	*Food crops*	*Animal husbandry*

List the major specific items transferred from one side of the world to the other:

	Diseases	Food Crops	Animals
From New To Old			
From Old to New			

Pic 561: In *Guns, Germs and Steel,* UCLA professor Jared Diamond crafted out a thesis that it was germs that did most of the damage, even more than guns and steel (swords), during the Spanish conquest of Mexico and Peru. Does this image support or argue against that thesis? Why do you say that?

The two crops from America that most augmented European diets were:	The three crops from America that most augmented Chinese diets were:

This recreational product from America is rolled and smoked in a pipe:

This recreational product from China became a fixture at British midday:

This recreational product from the Middle East elevated people's heart rates:

Columbian Exchange

Mercantilism

'Mother country'

Pic 565: Latin America is the most genetically mixed population in the world. While lineal descendants of Europeans exist, they make up a small fraction of the population except in places like Argentina and parts of Brazil. They form an elite class in Mexico, Peru and a few other places. Lineal descendants of African slaves live in Latin America too, and in fact predominate in Haiti, Jamaica and on some smaller Caribbean islands, while living as a minority group in Brazil, the Dominican Republic, Puerto Rico, Cuba and other places. The majority of the Latin American population is either Native American, lineal descendants of the Aztec, Inca and Mayan populations, or mestizo, a mix of Native American and European. When Cortes' Spanish soldiers married Native American elite women, this group was born, now the majority of those living in Mexico:

a. Spaniards *b. American Indians* *c. Mestizos* *d. Creoles*

Encomienda

Repartimiento

Hacienda

Peons

Creoles

Peninsulares ____

Circle two: In **Spain**, men generally tried to limit Spanish women marrying and producing offspring with:

a. African men *b. Jewish men* *c. Muslim men* *d. Mexican Indian men*

Circle two: In **New Spain**, men generally tried to limit Spanish women marrying and producing offspring with:

a. African men *b. Jewish men* *c. Muslim men* *d. Mexican Indian men*

Mestizo ____

Castas ____

Mestizas ____

Tupac Amaru revolt ____

Pic 569: The major cash crop that drove the Atlantic slave trade at first was ________________

Mulattoes ____

Snapshot 570: Note the percentages of the following:

	Spanish America	*Portuguese America (Brazil)*
European		
Mestizo		
African		
Native American		

While the race of a person was a big determiner of that person's social status in places like Brazil, how did their job in society also play a role if they had unique achievements? Give an example:

____

Unlike the Spanish and Portuguese settlers in Latin America, English settlers in North America largely came, at first, to:

a. escape religious persecution *b. make a new life* *c. both of these*

Demographically, British North America was different than Spanish America in the sense that:

a. Less Europeans came to settle *b. More Europeans came to settle*

____

By focusing on reading the Bible directly rather than listening to a priest's interpretation of it, Protestants in North America:

a. raised their literacy rate *b. had the same rates as Latin Americans*

What about the Russian environment made it an 'unlikely' place for a great and vast empire to spring forth from?

'Soft gold'

Tsar

Yasak

During this century, Russian migration east made them the majority group in Siberia: ___________

Map 574: Siberia has huge rivers not often studied or mentioned because many of them flow through tundra and vast unpopulated wilderness areas. Sketch them in the space below and label. Don't bother with the country boundaries etc., just the river shapes. The first river (going east to west) is the *Kolyma* (unlabeled on your map). To this should be added the *Amur* (which is the modern Chinese border), the *Lena*, the *Angara* (unlabeled- starts in Lake Baikal, flows through the city of Irkutsk, and meets the Yenisey, the *Yenisey*, the *Ob*, the *Irtysh* (unmarked- flows north from the Ural Mountains to the Barents Sea), the *Volga* (goes through Samara and empties at Astrakhan into the Caspian Sea, the *Dvina* (unlabeled- goes through the city of Archangelsk), the *Don* (unlabeled- starts south of Moscow, empties in the Azov Sea), and the *Dnieper* (unlabeled- goes through Smolensk and Kiev before emptying into the Black Sea).

Kolyma

Dnieper

Lake Baikal
(Crescent moon shape)

Map 574: Siberia is the vast expanse of land in the Russian Empire's *a. East* *b. West*

Pic 575: What class of Russian society did the fearsome Cossacks come from? ________________

Yermak

Peter the Great

'Window to the West'

What helps explain why after the New World was lost to the European imperial powers, Russia managed to hold onto their large land-based empire?

| What year did the 'empire' finally collapse?

Manchus

Qing dynasty

Pic 578 and Map 579: Machang, shown here, was instrumental in adding which three outlying provinces, formerly steppe and Himalayan mountain realms, to the Qing empire?

Looking at the map, predict which expanding power China will lose land to in the 19th century:

Court of Colonial Affairs

Mughals

Akbar

Sati

The sati ritual brings up an interesting point. When the British conquered India in the 18th century, they labeled it 'barbaric' and outlawed it. Now, that doesn't mean it didn't continue to go on in rural areas outside British supervision. Some say it still goes on today on occasion. If you were a lawyer arguing both sides of the case, what would your main points be?

The British should not have forced the Indians to change their culture, even though they found the practice of voluntary live cremation horrific

| *The British were right to impose their own values on India, because the idea of voluntary cremation really IS horrific!*

Nur Jahan

Shaykh Ahmad Sirhindi

Aurangzeb

Summarize how Aurangzeb's religious policies differed from those of Akbar:

Akbar's: *Aurangzeb's:*

Map 583: The empire of the past which the Ottomans destroyed that most resembles their empire- in the sense of the territorial rule they had over the Eastern Mediterranean- was this:

a. Athenian *b. Byzantine* *c. Holy Roman* *d. Russian*

Devshirme

Pic 585: The Ottomans were the most successful invaders of Europe in history. The Persians tried, Carthage tried, the Arabs tried, the Mongols tried, but all failed in the end until the Ottomans. Recall, their way was opened by the Seljuq Turks at the Battle of Manzikert (1071), back in Chapter 17. This battle convinced the Byzantine emperor to appeal to the Pope for help, and the result was the Crusades. After the Crusades, a second wave of Turks arrived, the Ottomans. Battles against them were legendary, and though they were eventually overthrown by the various nations under their control- namely Greeks, Bulgarians, Serbs, Croats, Hungarians, Wallachian Romanians and others- to this day a small corner of Europe, the Greek province of Thrace, is part of Turkey, not to mention Constantinople. Osman himself first defeated the Byzantines at Nicomedia (1337), but they were not ready to bring down Constantinople yet, so they went around it and defeated the Serbs at Kosovo (1389), the Bulgarians at Nicopolis (1396), had an amazing showdown at Varna (1444) where they defeated the combined Christian forces of Janos Hunyadi of Hungary, Vlad Dracula of Wallachia and King Wladyslaw of Poland, whose head they put on a spear and raised in celebration. Never good when your king (or president's) head is on a spear. Only then came the destruction of Byzantium and the fall of Constantinople (1453), but it didn't end there. What happened at the gates of Vienna in 1683?

Vienna was the farthest the Ottomans would get into Europe. Which centuries can be said to have witnessed the apex of Ottoman power?

a. 15th and 16th *b. 17th and 18th* *c. 19th and 20th*

Europeans were so relieved at the victory over the Ottomans at Vienna, that they honored the King of Poland, Jan Sobieski, who led the European forces, by naming a new constellation in the heavens. Look up the constellation *Scutum* (Latin for 'Shield'). Why do you think they named it that?

Zooming In 587: After reading the selection, answer the analysis questions that follow:

1)

2)

If you don't study hard, you're going to get the kind of luau they have Captain Cook- the second time.

Pic 600: This image tells us:

a. Africans were complicit in enslaving other Africans

b. Europeans enslaved Africans alone

The African-American woman who, in the opening vignette, visited Africa to see where her ancestors may have been taken from the coast, visited, like many do, this country:

____

Vasco da Gama

List some spices that were sought out as trade goods by Da Gama and the European explorers:

List some *other* goods that were sought as well:

Prester John

Map 604: Which European merchant ships ported at the following destinations?

Swahili Coast:

Goa, India:

Luanda, Ndongo:

Ceylon (Sri Lanka):

Malacca:

The Indies:

The Philippines:

Moluccas:

'Trading-post empire'

Pic 606: Where is Marco Polo in this scene?

What is he doing in this scene?

The authors write that the Portuguese Empire, despite being first in the region and first in trade, lost out because it became 'overextended.' What do you think that means in this context?

Philip II

Ferdinand Magellan

Manila

Dutch East India Company

British East India Company

This major island in the Pacific experienced 'co-colonization' by the Dutch and Chinese:

Pic 609: What symbols of British supremacy are findable in this famous image of the relationship between the BEIC and the colonial territories of the East?

Shogun

Tokugawas

The Tokugawa shoguns: *a. opened the country to trade* *b. mostly closed Japan to trade*

Map 612: On the way to the Mexico, the *Manila Galleons* carrying the silver from Potosi left via *this* city on the west coast of Peru:

Which city on the west coast of Mexico did the silver leave on its way to the Spanish Philippines & China?

List some methods of population control the Japanese employed during the Tokugawa era:

Zooming In 614: After reading the selection, answer the analysis questions that follow:

1)

If one were to ask you to link the rise in demand for fur hats and coats with the weather of the 17th century, what would you say?

The fur craze of the 17th century fueled a huge trade that went in many directions to many destinations. Note the ultimate destination of the furs trapped and sold in the following areas:

__________ *Kodiak & New Archangel* __________ *Fort Churchill*

__________ *Detroit & Montreal* __________ *Boston*

Smallpox

How did the introduction of alcohol have a similar effect on Native American societies as the introduction of new diseases did?

Pic 619: The Russian delegation visiting the Holy Roman Empire most likely encountered:

a. English *b. Germans* *c. French* *d. Romans*

We know the Portuguese were the first Europeans to sail around Africa. In the wake of Dias and Da Gama, the Arab slavers working the Swahili Coast of the continent were put out of business, and the kind of slave catching that brought perhaps | ____________________ | Africans to America over three centuries shifted to the west coast.

A comparable number (12,000,000) additional slaves were taken from East Africa in the earlier Islamic slave. trade. Add these to find the total number of Africans estimated to have been removed from the region to another continent between 600 and 1900:

____

Slavery is a thing of the past,
There is none in modern times: *T* *F*

The Muslim slave trade in white Europeans also ran into the millions. Add 2.5 million villagers captured from the Black Sea to 1.25 million captured from Italian and Spanish seacoast towns by the Barbary (Berber) Pirates of North Africa, for a total of:

____________________ Europeans enslaved.

Map 621: The place that saw the largest number of Africans by volume was this sugarcane producing colony:

a. The American South *b. Europe* *c. Mexico* *d. Brazil*

The word 'slave' comes from this European group:

a. Latins *b. Germanic* *c. Slavic*

Why were some Africans eager to sell other Africans to Arab and European slave trading companies?

What did Ibn Khaldun say to justify the Arab enslavement of Africans?

Pic 625: Triangular trade dealt in guns, people and cash crops. use arrows to show the direction of the trade, and which item was traded on that leg:

Europe

Americas

Africa

Snapshot 627: In which decade did the slave trade peak?	In which decade did it dramatically lessen?

Using the figures for total number to each particular destination in the second graph, rank them:

	DESTINATION	*NUMBER*	*PERCENTAGE OF TOTAL*
1			
2			
3			
4			
5			

Maize

Manioc

Lemba cult

Signares

Queen Nzinga

Zooming In 630: After reading the selection, answer the analysis questions that follow:

1)

2)

Copernicus stopped the sun and moved the earth.

Pic 642: How did Juan Diego in 1531 affect the cultural landscape of Mexico?

The authors write that Christianity, a European belief system, became a true world religion at this time in history. Where did it diffuse to?

The authors argue that after 1453 and even 1529, the future seemed to belong to the Islamic world not Europe. But sometimes the underdog scores at just the right time. Even so, what new divisive issue struck European Christendom in 1517?

Martin Luther

Ninety-Five Theses

Indulgences

Pic 646: Luther, a pious monk with a serious demeanor, who believed Christians should act Christian- meaning with charity and unselfishness- is dressed:

a. in ornate, beautiful garb that was probably very expensive *b. in a simple cloak*

*See how the men on the left in the fancy clothes are looking at each other in an agitate way? They are not agitated that Luther is posting his theses- the artist is foreshadowing how the people who followed Luther in his protest against the Catholic Church would become so angry they would go beyond even the reforms Luther asked for, and break away altogether to start the new denomination of Christianity called Lutheranism.

Is there a Lutheran church in your community? *a. Yes, I'm sure* *b. Maybe...* *c. I don't think so*

Snapshot 647: Summarize the positions of Catholics vs. Protestants on the major issues:

	Catholic perspective	***Protestant perspective***
Religious authority		
Role of the pope		
Ordination of clergy		
Salvation		
Status of Mary		

Snapshot cont.	***Catholic perspective***	***Protestant perspective***
Prayer		
Holy Communion		
Role of clergy		
Role of saints		

Map 648: Note whether the following 1) *converted* to a form of Protestantism, 2) *remained* mostly Catholic (green), or became religiously 3) *mixed* (mostly light orange) during the Reformation:

______________ *Ireland*	______________ *Scotland*	______________ *Switzerland*
______________ *England*	______________ *Spain*	______________ *Northern Germany*
______________ *Baltics*	______________ *Italy*	______________ *Southern Germany*
______________ *Poland*	______________ *France*	______________ *Scandinavia*

* ed. note: 'Germany' is within the center area of the Holy Roman Empire's boundaries, north of Swiss, west of Bohemia

---

How did Luther use Johann Gutenberg's new invention- the printing press- to further the message of Protestantism?

List other Protestant denominations:

St. Bartholomew's Day (8/24/72)

Edict of Nantes

Thirty Years' War

Peace of Westphalia

Counter-Reformation

Council of Trent

Jesuit Order

Map 651: The center of the Christian world as of 1500 was: *a. America* *b. Europe* *c. Asia*

Christianity did not diffuse to the following during the colonial era: *a. Central Asia* *b. India*

Puritans

Missionaries

In the past, we've spoken of Christianity as a universal religion like Buddhism and Islam, and unlike ethnic religions such as Judaism and Hinduism. But now, we have to clarify that. Catholic Christianity is always seeking converts and is always universalistic, which is why French and Spanish Catholics brought the Christian message to the Native Americans. Some Protestant denominations are also universal in their message, and are evangelistic too. Others, however, such as the Puritans (Pilgrims) practiced more of an ethnic Christianity. How is that reflected in their dealings with the Native Americans?

In ancient times, the city-states that fought in Mesopotamia believed that the city gods of the winning side were more powerful than the city gods of the losing side, and the losers adopted the gods of the winners because, well, they were better. Until some greater gods came around like Marduk, chief god of the Babylonians, who was more powerful still. Marduk was known far and wide *because* the Babylonians were so powerful. Was the concept that 'adopting the gods of the winning side is a good idea' reflected in the meeting of Europeans and Native Americans? How so?

Pic 653: What are the uniquely South American (Andean) elements in this version of the famous Last Supper?

Zooming In 655: After reading the selection, answer the analysis questions that follow:

1)

Taki Onqoy

Huacas

Cofradias

Matteo Ricci

How did Ricci and other missionaries in China use scientific breakthroughs in Europe to help get them an audience with high-ranking official at the Ming and Qing courts?

Pic 658: The word 'map' in Dutch is 'kaart,' and in German it is 'karte'. So, what do you think a cartographer does?

Are there any religious symbols on this scientific image of a map?

Why did some Chinese find European monogamous marriage *immoral*?

Rate the overall success of the Dutch and other European missionaries in bringing Christianity to China:

What were some distinctively African aspects of the *syncretic* forms of Christianity practiced by Africans in the Americas, like Voudou, Santeria and Candomble?

How did Islam differ in the following places from the more orthodox practices of the Middle East?

Aceh, Sumatra *Java*

What did the following do to fight syncretism and 'restore' what they saw as a pure Islam?

Aurangzeb *al-Wahhab*

Ibn Saud

Map 661: The Wahhabist movement was warmly welcomed in Ottoman territories: *a. T* *b. F*

Wang Yangming

Kaozheng

Cao Xueqin

Bhakti movement

Mirabi

Pic 663: Guru Nanak founded this religious movement in India: ____________________

Golden Temple

What factors did Europeans develop over time which helped spur on the Scientific Revolution?

Natural philosophy

Nicholas Copernicus

Johannes Kepler

Galileo

Blaise Pascal

Do you have a boring math teacher? Not as boring as Mr. Kepler. Dude straight up turned around and did complex math on the board for his own purposes, figuring out if Copernicus' theory was right, while his students just stared, puzzling over what the heck was going on. He got fired eventually, and that's when he went to seek out Tycho Brahe in Bohemia. Why? Because Brahe had the best star charts in Europe, and Kepler needed to know *exactly* where the planets were each night, to see if Copernicus was correct about the Sun being in the center and everything orbiting it. When Kepler, a serious and straightedge guy, got to Brahe's estate, he was angry because Brahe was having a feast and everyone was sitting around a huge table getting wasted and telling jokes. At the end of the night they passed out, got up, and did it all over again the next day. Brahe even had a gold-plated nose, and when Kepler asked why, he said, "A nobleman cut off the tip of my nose in a duel!" Could *this* guy really have the best star charts? Turns out he could, because Mr. Party Animal was serious about one thing- making an atlas of the sky. His charts were spot on. And when he finally presented them to Kepler, and Kepler plugged in the math, he realized that Copernicus' heliocentric idea was indeed right. The earth really does move. So, why didn't Copernicus' math fit? Kepler realized Copernicus' calculation error was that he assumed the orbits of the planets were nice, perfect circles. Brahe's data allowed Kepler to remap the sky and find out they were actually oval-shaped ellipses. You might study Kepler's *Laws of Planetary Motion* in science class. When you do, remember to tell your science teacher that he got the data for the theory from a drunk swashbuckler with a gold nose. Draw an oval below and put a little dot for the sun in the middle, and four 'earths' at different points around the oval.

Now, use Kepler's laws to write a little **F** next to the 'earth' that is moving the fastest, and an **S** next to the one moving slowest:

Isaac Newton

Rene Descartes

Zooming In 668: After reading the selection, answer the analysis questions that follow:

1)

Pic 670: In 1640, the great astronomer Johann Hevelius in Danzig on the Baltic seacoast was finishing the finest observatory of the 17th Century, shown in this image. Built on top of his home, which he called *Gwiezdne Miasto* ('Star Town'), its centerpiece was the world's largest telescope (50x magnification). Practicing astronomy was no easy task either- you had to invent your own tools when need be. Hevelius designed and built his own instruments; some based on those of his friend Tycho Brahe, the gold nose guy, who was working in Prague. Astronomers helped each other too. Sir Edmund Halley in England, for example (the Halley's Comet discoverer), sent Hevelius some of his own special telescope lenses that he made. Throughout the wars that plagued 17th Century Poland, including a huge revolt in the east that helped create a separate national identity for the Ukrainian people (vis-à-vis the Russians and Poles), Hevelius and his friends catalogued the sky, systematizing the constellations. He produced books about comets, the lunar surface, and a sky atlas- all containing precise measurements, drawings and data. Hevelius also built a solar telescope to get a better look at sunspots, by projecting the Sun's image into a dark room. Galileo had done something similar in Italy a few decades earlier. In *Machina Coelestis* (1673), Hevelius' observatory was described as having "three wooden walls and a canvas (or leather) curtain wall that rolls up for observing," with the room itself being, "wheel-mounted and rotatable to face a celestial object." One of his prized tools was a "quadrant made of copper, with an iron frame, engraved with portraits of Hipparchus, Ptolemy, Copernicus, and Tycho Brahe." Many of Hevelius' tools were plated in gold, to guard against the salt air coming off the Baltic. When King Jan III Sobieski ascended the throne, he not only fought back the Turks at Vienna, but in more peaceful times also patronized his favorite astronomer, visiting the observatory many times. The king's patronage proved especially important in 1679, when a fire destroyed the whole house and the observatory had to be totally rebuilt. When it was done, Hevelius was an old man, but he did not forget his king's help: when it fell to him to name a new constellation, he's the guy who made sure that over their heads would now fly, forevermore, the constellation *Scutum Sobiescanum*: The Shield of Sobieski. If you had a flat roof on your house, what would you do with the space there? Would you build a telescope like Hevelius?

Royal Society

Giordano Bruno

Adam Smith

How did Immanuel Kant define *Enlightenment*?

John Locke

Voltaire

Voltaire believed God had made:

a. just the Earth *b. many worlds in the heavens above*

Pic 672: Voltaire and other *philosophes* met in salons like these. How is this salon different than a salon that a woman might visit today?

Enlightenment meaning of the term: *Modern usage of the term:*

Emilie du Chatelet, like her father, used her large chateau as a *salon,* a place in which philosophical discussions amongst large groups of *philosophes* might take place. They talked about politics and science mostly, but history was not a popular subject. Back then, not many people studied it. Certainly it wasn't taught it in school as a 'subject', and even if it had been, most kids didn't go to school in 1740. She hated the subject of World History especially, and if you have World History you might know why. She said it was "just a jumble of names and dates, very illogical, and unstructured." But Voltaire disagreed. He had a vision of a way World History could be thought that would *not* be boring, and became determined to find her a book that she would like. He couldn't. Let Voltaire describe what happened:

"I said to her, 'If, in this vast amount of raw material you were able to select that which would allow you to build something valuable for your own use; if you omitted the details of each war, which are as boring as they are uncertain; if you omitted all the small negotiations which turned out to be useless treachery; all the particular incidents which obliterate the greater events; if indeed you could turn this chaos into a general and definite picture, teasing out the ***story of the human mind*** *from these events, do you think THAT would be a waste of your time?' And lo, the idea won her over. This plan guided my thoughts to the idea of writing such a world history book myself. I was surprised how little the multitude of books already existing would help."* After this exchange, Voltaire likely decided to:

a. read her an existing book *b. write one for her himself*

Deist

Pantheist

How did the following Europeans of the Enlightenment era describe their favorite subject: women?

Encyclopedia writers *Jean-Jacques Rousseau*

How did the following European women react to these opinions?

Madame Beaulmer *Mary Wollstonecraft*

Marquis de Condorcet

The Inner Light

Social Gospel

Charles Darwin

Natural Selection

Karl Marx

Sigmund Freud

What is 'Dutch Learning' and where could it be 'exchanged' in Japan?

No army can stop an idea whose time has come.

Pic 696: Anyone in your class taking French? See if they can translate this:

Above the pic: Vive le Roi, Vive la Nation:

Under the pic:

According to this image, the French Revolution:

a. Elevated the class status of the 1st Estate (Royals and High clergy)

b. Elevated the class status of the 2nd Estate (Nobles)

c. Elevated the class status of the 3rd Estate (Peasants)

Note what was going on in the following world regions as the Atlantic world stood on the brink of revolution:

Safavid Persia	*Mughal India*	*Wahhabi Arabia*
Czarist Russia	*West Africa*	*Southern Africa*

The consequences of the Seven Years' War set the conditions for the Atlantic revolutions. What was the major reason why?

List some core Enlightenment ideas:

Popular sovereignty

John Locke

The Social Contract

Why have the Atlantic revolutions been often referred to as 'democratic revolutions'?

Can a simple button change the course of history? Back when he was a young 'Redcoat,' in 1755 during the French and Indian War, George Washington's button saved his life. Washington's men under General Braddock were ambushed from the trees (the exact same tactics the Patriots under Washington would later use in the Revolutionary War), and Ol' Georgie was moving across the battlefield relaying Braddock's orders. He was shot at by a hail of musket fire. Then he was shot at again, and again and again. In fact, every other mounted officer that did this was killed in the flurry of ambush *except* Washington. Two horses were shot out from under him, but he remounted each time and continued to do his duty. As 700 men fell to their deaths, and with destruction all around him, by some amazing circumstance, Washington survived. He wrote as much to his brother John, "I had been protected beyond all human probability or expectation; for I had four bullets through my coat, and two horses shot under me, yet escaped unhurt, although death was leveling my companions on every side." Unbeknownst to Washington, the special gold seal button he wore on his uniform, which bore the initials G.W., was later found. Why was it on the ground? It had a bullet hole in it. How much value do you *personally* place in providential pieces of history like Washington's button?

Would you ever consider buying an antique from the time, or an old coin from the era, on *Ebay*?

a. Yeah that would be cool *b. Probably not*

Would you ever consider getting an old copy of the Declaration of Independence, framing it, and putting it up in the entranceway of your house?

a. Oh yeah, that's America baby! *b. You're kidding, right?*

Map 702: After the American Revolution, the thirteen colonies became the thirteen states of America, with a lower-case 's' for 'states'. When the states each ratified the Constitution, they became United States. Rank the thirteen states by their land area:

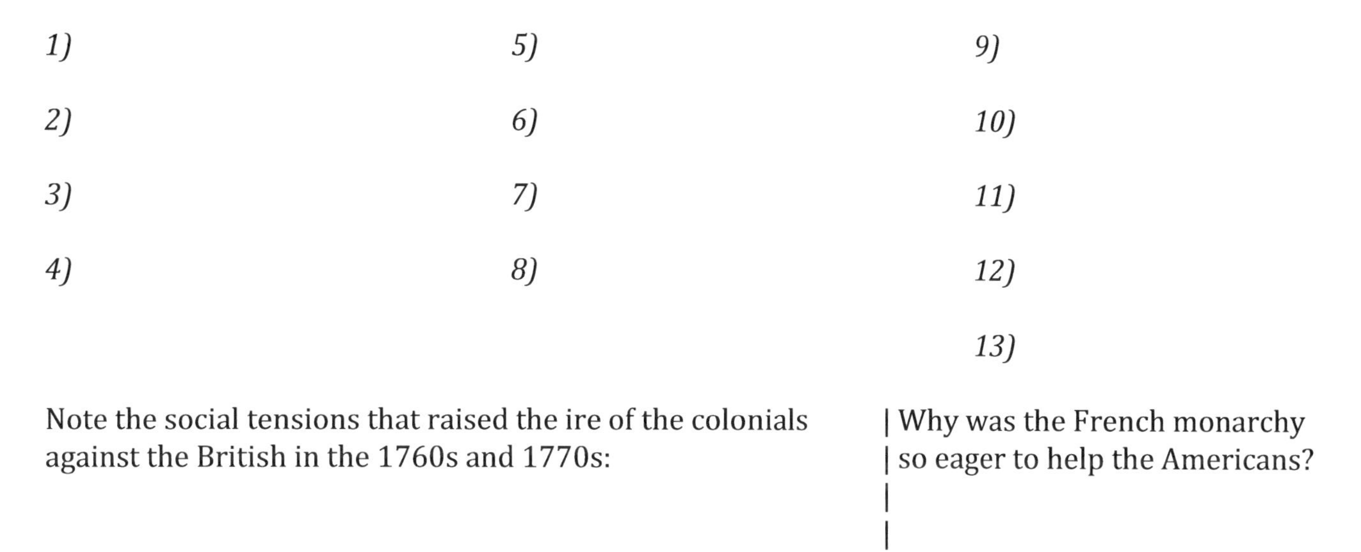

1) *5)* *9)*

2) *6)* *10)*

3) *7)* *11)*

4) *8)* *12)*

13)

Note the social tensions that raised the ire of the colonials against the British in the 1760s and 1770s:

Why was the French monarchy so eager to help the Americans?

Ever heard the story of the Midnight Ride of Paul Revere? At Old North Church in Boston, a historical landmark today, Revere conspired with a maintenance worker who worked at the church to light one lantern in the belfry as a signal to the Patriots that the Redcoats were marching by land, and to light two if they were crossing over the river- 'by sea'- and assembling on the other shore before moving out to Lexington and Concord. He waited and got the signal- two lanterns. They shined for less than a minute, so the British would not think anything of it if someone noticed. Revere and two others were off to warn the <u>*Patriots*</u> and everyone else on the way to Lexington and Concord beyond, that:

A. *Hey y'all can go stain some silver or go back to bed y'all* B. *The British are coming!*

After a century of independence, the United States was the world's most _______________ country.

a. Monarchical *b. Aristocratic* *c. Democratic* *d. Dictatorial*

Got a dollar bill in your pocket? Alright, hand it over! Actually, yeah get it out and check out the symbols on the back. Eighteenth century America was variously called a *New Arcadia*, a *New Athens*, and by the Pilgrim Fathers 200 years earlier, a *New Jerusalem*. John Edwards even called Americans a 'new chosen people' and there could be no doubt: in Christian America, progress was felt to be divine. The country's existence was seen as ushering in a new stage of providential history. The name of the capital city of the state of Rhode Island will tell you that. Much is made by conspiracy theorists about the symbols printed on American money, especially on the one-dollar bill. What could be the meaning of the unfinished pyramid with the capstone levitating above it? What do the Latin phrases such as *Novus ordo seclorum* really mean? The phrase comes from the Roman writer Virgil, and means, 'A New Order of the Ages.' Virgil may have written in pre-Christian Roman times, but his age was seen by both pagan and Christian Romans as a Golden Age, for it was the Age of Augustus *and* the age in which Christ walked in the far outpost of Galilee. Medieval Christians later read poets like Virgil and often saw them as the inspired crafters of socially positive messages, even as sources of revelation. They lived in an age of meaning, as the early Americans did. *Seclorum* here does not mean secular, but rather (like the French *siècle*) 'age'. The whole phrase together signifies 'The New Age of America,' begun in the year blazoned on the base of the pyramid, on its foundation stones: MDCCLXXVI. The pyramid is unfinished because the American national project, which is religious and secular at the same time, and which is at the head of the Enlightenment and modernist project of civilization as a whole, is unfinished. It goes on, defining progress before the eyes of all. *Annuit Coeptis* tells us Providence both guides and approves the undertaking of the project. The eagle on the front holds the olive branches of peace in one talon and the arrows of war in the other, but its face is turned to the side of the olive branch, showing its preference. American colors also have their meaning: red (hardiness and valor), is merged with white (purity and innocence) and blue (perseverance and justice). What year is MDCCLXXVI?

___

Federalist Papers ___

Louis XVI ___

Estates General ___

Declaration of the Rights of Man ___

Ancien Regime ___

French Revolution ___

Jean-Jacques Rousseau ___

National Assembly ___

Pic 705: What is this murder device, which, perhaps ironically, was built specifically to make executions more quick and humane:

Why did the execution of King Louis and Queen Marie shock traditionalists?

___

Maximilian Robespierre ___

Revolutionary calendar ___

Some countries don't have an independence day- because they were never ruled by a foreign power. Britain is one, France is another. So they celebrate July 14 as Bastille Day. What happened?

___

Olympe de Gouges

Festival of Unity

If you visited France today and saw that the Cathedral of Notre Dame had all the crosses and Christian items removed, and someone told you, "Hey didn't you hear? That's now the Temple of Reason," would you:

a. Be glad the old religion was gone *b. Be disturbed at the change* *c. Not care that much*

Napoleon

Map 708: Place the appropriate year next to the event. As a general, Napoleon fought the British and Ottomans in Egypt, at the Battle of the Pyramids, Battle of the Nile and Aboukir Bay. Then, as First Consul, he consolidated rule over France, and, after declaring himself emperor, he then defeated the Austrians, Prussians and Russians at: ***Austerlitz, Ulm*** and ***Jena***. He then moved on Iberia, winning at ***Salamanca*** in Spain, but he did lose a major naval battle to Admiral Lord Nelson, the ***Battle of Trafalgar.*** In which year did this lose take place?

____

At the zenith of his military conquests, Napoleon had most of Europe under his control or allied with him in some way. What states were still at war with France (check the map key):

After six years of rule, Napoleon fought the ***Russian Campaign*** in Moscow in ________________, but lost big due to the Czar's Scorched Earth Policy, Cossack attacks, and lack of winter supplies.

On the way back from the disastrous retreat, the 'nominal allies' on the map gathered and fought France at the Battle of the Nations: also called ***Leipzig*** in the year:

After this loss, Napoleon abdicated the throne and was exiled, but escaped from Elba and returned for a Hundred Days, fought, but lost at: the ***Battle of Waterloo*** in this year:

Saint-Domingue

At right, sketch out a triangle and place in it the hierarchies of Haitian society during the colonial era, labeling the number of people in each caste, from top to bottom:

1) Grand blancs
2) Petit blancs
3) Gens de couleur
4) Slaves

Grand blancs ________________________

Petit blancs ________________________

Gens de couleur libres ________________________

Why did black slaves on Haiti revolt in 1791 and what were the consequences?

Reasons: *Consequences:*

____

Toussaint Louverture ________________________

Jean-Jacques Dessalines ________________________

Pic 710: Remember how the Aztecs crumbled around the Spanish due to smallpox as much or more than due to Spanish guns and swords? If the Conquistadors had an invisible ally in the 16th century, in the 19th century in Haiti, it was the Africans who had invisible allies against the Europeans. Malaria and Yellow Fever, tropical diseases the Europeans had little or no defenses against, struck Napoleon's troops, ultimately forcing them to withdraw from the island. What happened to the whites remaining after Dessalines declared Haiti America's 'Black Republic?'

____

"Remember Haiti" ________________________

Creoles ________________________

Hidalgo-Morales rebellion ________________________

Tupac Amaru ________________________

Map 712: Note the Latin American colonies that won independence in the following years:

1804 ________________

1811 ________________

1816 ________________

1817 ________________

1818 ________________

1819 ________________

1821 ________________

1822 ________________

1823 ________________

1824 and after ________________

Pic 713: Simon Bolivar's dream was of *Gran Colombia,* a kind of United States of South America, based on the Anglo-American example. Why was it difficult for him and San Martin to craft out a new *Americano* identity in South America that included all *casta* divisions based on race and class?

____

Constitutions are cool! The cry for constitutions based on classical liberal political values rang out in Europe after the end of the French Revolution, when the Congress of Vienna set the continent back on a conservative monarchist track in 1815. In which three years did social revolution erupt?

Pic 715: During the 18th and 19th centuries, Christians in Europe and America tended to

a. show their support for continuing the slave system *b. increasingly became voices for abolition*

Great Jamaica Revolt

Freetown

Zooming In 717: After reading the selection, answer the analysis questions that follow:

1)

Why was West African chieftain Osei Bonsu upset that the British would no longer buy his slaves?

Just as blacks in America became an emancipated group, the serfs of Russia were emancipated by the Czar. Describe how the situations of both these groups were different:

American blacks: *Russian serfs:*

Levee en masse

Nationalism

What kinds of things are national identity based on? Draw a graphic organizer with 'nation' in the center and your factors that go into national identity emerging from that center:

How did nationalism affect the following groups in the 19th century?

Germans and Italians	*Serbs and Greeks*	*Czechs and Hungarians*
Poles and Ukrainians	*Irish*	*Jews*

Which emerging nations were involved in the War of the Triple Alliance in South America?

Map 721: The goal of nationalism is to secure an independent national territory and state that reflects the self-determination of the national group. In the 19th century, many European nations of people were 'trapped' in larger empires dominated by their neighbors, and wished to have their own states. Each of the following pairs contains one European nation that was 'free', and another which was 'trapped.' Identify which was which using the map clues and circle the 'free' nation:

Great Britain / Ireland *Poland / Russia* *Ottoman Empire / Croatia*

Czech / Austria *Spain / Norway* *Greece / Macedonia*

If the nationalist feelings are more associated with the geographical territory and the race of the people is less of the focus, this is called:

a. civic nationalism *b. ethnic nationalism*

Pic 722: Because the Poles shown here were fighting the Russians as cultural and political outsiders dominating their people, who wanted free expression of their ethnic 'Polishness,' was their nationalism more civic or ethnic? Why?

How did nationalism express itself outside Europe in the following places:

Egypt	*Japan*	*India*

Vindication of the Rights of Women

Seneca Falls Conference

Elizabeth Cady Stanton

Florence Nightingale

Jane Addams

Pic 725: What were the goals these women were marching for?

Zooming In 726: After reading the selection, answer the analysis questions that follow:

1)

Say you were doing a project on the Women's / Feminist movement and protests worldwide. Using pages 724-727, construct the following timeline of events your project might focus on:

1848

1852

1869

1879

1893

1900

1906

1913

1914

1923

1945

Remember, if you get lost on a deserted island, try to switch to inanimate sources of power as fast as you can. Then, it's hammock time!

Pic 736: Another famous painting of early Industrial Age factories called buildings like the ones shown, 'Satanic mills.' Wordsworth and Blake agree. Imagine walking from home to this area of Swansea to work. Think of four kinds of environmental issues that would likely confront you:

1) *2)*

3) *4)*

Unlike the Agricultural Revolution, which occurred independently in the riverine civilizations and select other places, the Industrial Revolution began in a certain country at a certain time, after 1750. What country was that?

Industry was driven by a move from sources of energy. *a. inanimate to animate* *b. animate to inanimate*

Guano

Anthropocene

'Culture of innovation'

List specific textile and steam-based machines that drove early industry:

1)

2)

3)

4)

5)

List specific later-19th century breakthroughs of various kinds that continued Age of Industry:

1)

2)

3)

4)

5)

Patent

Do you know how to locate the source of contentious points made in a textbook? In the debate about the origins of the Industrial Revolution and why it occurred in Europe, scholars used to agree in the majority with the person who is sourced in Ch. 17 note 4, whose argument is summarized on pg. 741.

What is this scholar's argument?

Source him by going to the back of the book. Copy his bibliographic information below:

The authors dispute the argument about Europe being in any way special by citing some innovations in other parts of the world. Summarize those innovations:

Islamic World	*India*	*China*

Summarize some of the reasons our authors believe helped allow Europe to pull ahead in industry, what scholars call, 'The Great Divergence':

Competition:

State-commercial relations:

Hub of a new commercial network:

Map 743: This country had the densest railroad network in 1850 ____________________

While this country had coalfields, it did not have a significant industrial area in 1850:

____

While this country had a significant industrial area around Milan, it didn't have much coal:

____

Note some agricultural innovations that helped British farmers become more productive- something that both freed up labor to do other kinds of jobs, and produced a greater population:

Note some ways the British political system encouraged industrialization:

The Royal Society

Note ways in which industrialization both destroyed and created:

What it destroyed	*What it created*

During the Age of Industry, the aristocratic landowning class *gained* *declined* in power.

During this age, the middle class tended to *gain* *decline* in relative power.

Note some occupations that emerged at this time that were considered middle class:	How did middle class people *behave* that was supposed to separate them from the working poor, according to Samuel Smiles and others?

'Respectability'

'Domesticity'

Note some occupations that emerged at this time that were considered lower middle class:	Pic 748: In our culture, middle class people tend to dress like the working class or even the underclass. Back then, it was a goal of middle class people to: *a. dress like their social betters* *b. dress like hooligans*

Note some occupations that emerged at this time that were considered laboring class jobs:	Pic 750: This image depicts bad water, one of the 7 problems facing city dwellers in the 19th century. What are the other six?

'Friendly societies'

Robert Owen

Karl Marx

Labour Party

Pic 754: The socialist program promoted by the Marxist International Publishing Company railed against the capitalist system in this image. What kind of feelings do you think it was supposed to engender by identifying social betters who 'eat for you', 'shoot at you', 'fool you' and 'rule you'?

The origin of the theory of communism provides a good opportunity to practice historical thinking. As the book says, Marx came from a family of Jewish origin living in Germany. His father changed his name from Hirschel to Heinrich to sound more German, and converted to Christianity. Both of these actions are examples of *assimilation* to a dominant culture, and the notion of oppression in society *by* the dominant culture is something that permeated Marx' analysis of the capitalist world order. In college in Berlin, Marx was introduced to the writings of Hegel, whose *Philosophy of History* identified the driving pattern of historical change as one of dialectical motion, beginning with an established 'thing' (thesis) that is challenged by its opposite (antithesis), which causes historical activity to follow, such as revolutionary violence, which blends both threads into a new order (synthesis). Marx took Hegel's concept of dialectical motion through time and hypothesized that *class conflict* throughout history provided a constant antithesis to what he viewed as an ever-present class-based order (the thesis), and caused struggle resulting, eventually, in a new synthesis. Each new historical synthesis, however, got perverted by class oppression again, triggering a new antithesis, and the cycle goes on. In Marxism, the bourgeoisie are the emerging middle class and capitalist oppressor class, such as the people pictured on the upper parts of pg. 754. The workers and peasants, meanwhile, are the proletarian class, which should realize their travails and rise up to overthrow the existing order and establish a new classless society (communism). After they do that, what should their social goals be, according to Marx?

Marx delivered the Communist Manifesto in the 1840s, but was dismayed that no communist society emerged, except for a brief flirtation in Paris in 1870 that flared out. Two phenomena are discussed by the authors that allow us to explain why no communist society emerged until the Soviet Union in 1917. What are some specific examples that illustrate each?

Capitalist wealth generation: *Nationalism:*

Settler colony

Map 756: If you live in the United States, Canada, Australia, New Zealand, Argentina or South Africa, you live in a European settler colony. But is that always going to be the case? European descendants in the settler colonies have tended to have low birth rates since around 1990. While they are still a majority in the countries listed above, they are *all* projected to become a minority in favor of non-Europeans with higher TFRs (total fertility rates, i.e.: the average number of children born per woman) during this century. UN population statistics forecast the transition to take place in the following years for the following countries:

United States of America: 2045
Canada: 2052
New Zealand: 2054
Australia: 2055
Great Britain: 2066

How old will you be when people of European descent are projected to become a minority in your country?

'Melting pot'

By the end of the 19th century, Russians made up about *a. 90%* *b. 10%* of Siberia's population.

Today, things are different. In the 21st century, 6 million Russians live in Siberia near the Chinese border, and they face over 90 million Chinese looking back at them across that border, according to Frank Jacobs, author of *Strange Maps*, writing in the New York Times (2014). Overall, the Russians are at a 10-1 population disadvantage against the Chinese in Siberia. Do you think China will subsume Siberia from Russia in this century?

Zooming In 758: After reading the selection, answer the analysis questions that follow:

1)

2)

Note the four largest producers of manufactured goods in the year 1914:

1)

2)

3)

4)

Map 761: Rank the states by the number of manufacturing cities they had in 1900 (don't count stars- just red dots! One state has 6, so start there):

American coal mining was concentrated in these regions of the country in 1900:

a. The West and the South *b. The Midwest and the Great Plains* *c. The Northeast and the South*

'Scientific management'

Mail-order catalog

Model T

Note some reasons socialism and Marxism didn't take hold very much amongst the *American* working class:

If the Western country furthest west (the USA) was the 'most free,' Russia, the Western country furthest east, was the 'most authoritarian'. What political institutions did it not have in this period that most other Western countries in Europe and in the settler colonies did?

Pic 763: You need to do an image search for Gustav Dore. Do you sketch? This guy was the master of sketching. He did all manner of mythical scenes, biblical scenes and other stuff. Judging by the picture here, was he a fan of Russian serfdom?

a. no *b. yes*

As Russia rapidly industrialized, many emancipated serfs quickly became radical laborers. Why might they have been so quick to form a class consciousness and embrace aspects of socialism while Americans of the working class rejected those same socialist principles in favor of individual work = individual success?

Revolution of 1905

Duma

Map 765: List the cities in the Russian Empire that had major strikes or military uprisings in 1905:

Warsaw is a Polish city that was conquered by the Russian Empire. Why don't you think a soviet formed there?

Bolshevik Party

Vladimir Lenin

Snapshot 767: Britain peaked in its industrial might in relation to the other powers in ________

Germany peaked *a. earlier* *b. at the same time* *c. later* than Great Britain.

China began declining after the year *a. 1750* *b. 1800* *c. 1850*

Caudillos

Haciendas

Which indigenous American people fought the creoles in the Caste War of the Yucatán?

Note the major export products of the following Latin American countries after independence:

Mexico	*Chile*	*Bolivia*	*Peru*	*Brazil*
Central America		*Argentina*	*Ecuador*	*Cuba*

Map 769: Rank the Latin American countries by the amount of money American businessmen invested in the economy- for better or worse- by 1914:

Country	*Amount in million of $*

While today there are restrictions on the number of Europeans that are allowed to migrate to the United States, Canada and other countries in the Americas, why did Latin American countries like Argentina, Uruguay and Brazil want to increase immigration from Europe in the 20th century?

Porfirio Diaz

Pic 771: During the Mexican Revolution, what was the role of women?

Pancho Villa

Emiliano Zapata

'Dependent development'

'Banana republics'

Reflections 773: Do you think history has a goal to which we should strive? Something like the colonization of space? What is it?

"That's a fine railroad you got there- must've been tough to build." "Thanks, but it was the white man's burden really. We just had to build it."

Pic 786: Answer the following for this representative image of the European imperial order.

Who:

What:

When:

Where:

Why:

How:

For what two reasons did the British in African colonies refrain from speaking too much English to the natives (hint: The Mongols of the Yuan Dynasty didn't speak Mongolian to the Chinese when they ruled China 600 years earlier for the same two reasons):

1) 2)

At the end of last chapter, a rundown of industrial and agricultural trade products from Latin America was presented. Now we have more countries and colonies in the world trade network to summarize:

West Africa *Ceylon* *South Africa* *Southeast Asia*

Cecil Rhodes

Cecil Rhodes left in his last will and testament a chunk of his fortune to establish a scholarship, the Rhodes Scholarship, to people who wanted to further Anglo-American cooperation and power. If Manifest Destiny sought to extend the sway of Anglo-Saxon America over the whole continent of North America, Rhodes sought to extend the sway of British imperial rule over all the *world*- which he argued would be in the best interests of the world, because British and Anglo-American organization was the best form of social order. See? Now you know, and that makes you a kind of Rhodes scholar too. Summarize the specific motives of imperialism:

Economic	Political	Cultural

Pic 790: Did the American comic artist who drew this approve or disapprove of British imperialism? Why do you think so?

Suez Canal

Quinine

In the Middle Ages, Europeans who met non-Europeans, such as M. Ricci or Marco Polo, would be most likely to draw this distinction with them:

a. they are heathen and we are Christian- if we bring them the Gospel they can probably achieve salvation like us

b. they are savage and we are civilized- but they can be taught and their level of culture can be improved

c. we are more highly evolved than the rest of humanity, and they are uncivilized because they are genetically inferior

During the Enlightenment era in the 18th century, Europeans like Voltaire and Rousseau would most likely draw this distinction between Europeans and non-Europeans:

a. they are heathen and we are Christian if we bring them the Gospel they can probably achieve salvation like us

b. they are savage and we are civilized- but they can be taught and their level of culture can be improved

c. we are more highly evolved than the rest of humanity, and they are uncivilized because they are genetically inferior

Pic 791: With the advent of evolution theory, which of the above answers do you think scientists in Europe and American began to use more and more to explain the growing difference in the relative power of Western Civilization as against all other cultures in the world?

____

'Yellow Peril'

'Child race'

What did British doctor Robert Knox say about race?

'Civilizing Mission'

By what actions did Europeans who believed in the Civilizing Mission think they could help the more primitive peoples of the world, many of whom now lived in colonies they controlled?

Social darwinism

Just as domesticators changed the characteristics of certain animals through many generations of selective breeding, turning wolves into various dog breeds and wild bulls into docile milk and meat producing moo-cows, European scientists like Francis Galton and Herbert Spencer began to believe they could improve the human stock by disallowing certain strains of people from having children, while encouraging people with what they considered 'positive' or 'desirable' traits to have an extra kid or two- even at public expense. In the end, the investment would be worth it, they argued, because the 'selected' people would be more likely to contribute to making a better society in the next generation. This trend in science is called *eugenics* (good genes). How do the authors employ the metaphor of the garden to illustrate this concept?

While in the first wave of European colonization focused on the Western Hemisphere (North and South America), where was the focus of the second?

On what did Hilaire Belloc believe the British could depend even in the face of hundreds of millions of colonials?

'Scramble for Africa'

Battle of Isandlwana

Boer War

Map 795: Note which territories in Asia were held by the following European powers:

Britain:

France:

Netherlands:

United States:

Japan:

Indian reservation

Liberia

How many African-Americans went back across the Atlantic to live in Liberia?

What happened when they got there?

What if a foreign corporation invaded your country with a private army? What corporation could do it? Microsoft? Apple? Ford? Toyota? Well that's what happened to the rump of Mughal India, after it split and a force commanded by the British East India Company started winning conflicts against local rulers, absorbing India into the British Empire state by state. The final battle was against the state of Mysore, where Tipu Sultan's force of 30,000 defenders was defeated by the BEIC's 'army' of 4,000 Brits and 40,000+ Indian mercenaries. So... if a foreign corporation invaded your country, what would you do? Collaborate for a good job or resist and be targeted?

Map 796: Note which territories in Africa were held by the following European powers:

Britain:

France:

Germany:

Italy:

Portugal:

Belgium:

Spain:

Independent states:

Which groups in the colonies tended to cooperate most with European rule?

Indian Rebellion

Why did the rebellion, also known as the Sepoy Rebellion or Indian Mutiny, begin?

Bwana

In a society where there was a lot of racial animosity, would you feel comfortable if the judge or jury hearing your case was made up of people of another race?

a. yes, it wouldn't bother me	Were British people living in India comfortable with it?
b. I would be uncomfortable	

'Homelands'

Apartheid

Why did Europeans administrators of colonial territories generally *disfavor* 'detribalization'?

'Statute labor'

Pic 803: Even today, according to Newsweek Magazine (*The World's Most Barbaric Punishments*, 7/8/2010), cutting off the right hand is a punishment in many countries:

"Right hands have been cut off at the wrist as punishment for theft in Sharia-controlled areas of Nigeria and in Saudi Arabia. Repeat offenders in the latter can lose both hands, and legs are sometimes taken for other offenses... In Iran, in early 2008, five robbers had their right hands and left feet cut off in one week- a practice known as cross amputation. According to The New York Times, *'doctors watched to limit bleeding and infection during the procedure.' Hands and feet are also cut off as punishment in Yemen, Sudan, and Somalia."*

What evidence of strict disciplinary measures can be seen in this image?

Leopold II

The authors blame European colonialism, which began a hundred years before AIDS appeared, and ended decades before it was first reported, as having caused or somehow facilitated the diffusion of the disease. Do you agree with this assessment?

Maji-Maji Rebellion

How did European rule affect the following Asian river valleys?

Irrawaddy Delta, Burma *Mekong Delta, Vietnam*

Pic 806: Is foreign direct investment (FDI) a blessing *and* a curse, or just one or the other? What is your opinion using this situation and another specific and valid example you think of?

Lipton in Ceylon: *Your example:*

'Squatters'

Why do you think life was so controlled for workers in South African diamond and gold mines?

Which societies enacted laws to end Chinese immigration in the late-19th century?

1) 2) 3) 4)

Summarize the kinds of jobs and roles women had in the following colonies:

Ghana:

Ivory Coast:

Cameroon:

Botswana:

South Africa:

Nigeria:

Zooming In 810: After reading the selection, answer the analysis questions that follow:

1)

Southern Rhodesia:

Thomas Malthus prophesized doom in his *Essay on Population* (1798). He argued population growth would be exponential, but the ability of the land to feed the greater number of people would only grow in a linear way. Thus, at some point, the number of people would outstrip the amount of food, and there would be mass famine. Though Malthus was worried most about his native Britain, where technological gains and out-migration to America helped prevent famine in the century that followed, India was hit many times, as Ireland was in the 1840s. In terms of population, India is the second largest country in the world after China, and may be number one by 2030. It was struck by all of the following:

1770	*Bengal Famine*	*10,000,000 deaths*	*1865*	*Orissa Famine*	*1,000,000 deaths*
1783	*Chalisa Famine*	*11,000,000 deaths*	*1869*	*Rajputana Famine*	*1,500,000 deaths*
1791	*Skull Famine*	*11,000,000 deaths*	*1876*	*Great Famine*	*6,000,000 deaths*
1837	*Agra Famine*	*800,000 deaths*	*1896*	*India Famine I*	*5,500,000 deaths*
1860	*Upper Doab Famine*	*2,000,000 deaths*	*1899*	*India Famine II*	*1,000,000 deaths*

The amount relief the British administration could have furnished to India to combat these mass famines is debatable, but the authors argue they could have changed the crops harvested and didn't. On the other hand, the British did emphasize modernization.

What is modernization?

Give three specific examples of modernization:

What did it mean to 'uplift native races'?

Pic 815: What evidence do you see here of adoption of European norms by native elites?

How did Christian missionaries react to and what did they teach native Africans on the following:

Female nudity:

Polygyny (marrying more than one person at a time):

Sexual acts outside of the marriage bond:

Western gender norms:

Female circumcision:

Note ways Christianity in Africa become 'Africanized' with animist additions or subtractions?

Pic 817: If you were in a class like this and everyone teaching you was from another country- as it seems these teachers are- but you considered that country more powerful and prosperous, do you think you would be more or less receptive to the message they were bringing?

Zooming In 818: After reading the selection, answer the analysis questions that follow:

1)

'Backsliding'

What did Senegalese scholar C.A. Diop argue that flipped the script on European assumptions about Africa's backward state?

What did Edward Blyden argue was good about African cultural norms?

Why do you think some pan-Africanists like Marcus Garvey started to argue around this time that blacks worldwide should embrace a greater racial identity instead of many tribal identities?

Student: "Why do they call it 'laissez-faire' capitalism if it was unfair?" Teacher: "The people who named it were just being laissez."

Pic 832: Who is carving the 'Chinese pie':

Representative *Country*

Modern leaders like Mao Zedong, Liu Shaoqi, Deng Xiaoping, Zhao Ziyang, Jiang Zemin, Hu Jintao and current leader Xi Jinping have emphasized the 'pain' caused by Britain to China in the 1800s. What was this humiliation?

Qianlong

'Celestial Empire'

The Manchus were part Chinese and part Mongol and Xiongnu by heredity- why were they often portrayed to the Han Chinese population as 'foreign leaders' by their foes?

Taiping Uprising

Hong Xiuquan

Hakka women

Pic 836: About how long did the Taiping rebellion, in which a shocking 25,000,000 people were killed, continue before the Qing rules retook the Taiping headquarters of Nanjing shown here?

Pic 839: These aristocrats are chillin' out smoking ________________, from which heroin is synthesized.

Snapshot 838: Without selling opium to the Chinese, the British would have run a big trade deficit due to their fondness for this other kind of 'leaf', which comes in green, white and black:

____

Lin Zexu

Opium War

Treaty of Nanjing

'Informal empire'

Zooming In 840: After reading the selection, answer the analysis questions that follow:

1)

2)

'Self-strengthening'

Boxer Uprising

Qiu Jin

Map 842: Which cities and rivers are in the following foreign spheres of influence areas in China?

Power	***Cities***	***Rivers***
Japan		
Russia		
Britain		
France		
Germany		

'Hundred Days'

'Sick Man of Europe'

Map 845: We can say, in general, that the Ottoman Empire	We can say, in general, that the Ottoman Empire	We can say, in general that the Ottoman Empire
gained lost neither	*gained lost neither*	*gained lost neither*
European land in the 19th century.	African land in the 19th century.	its land in the Middle East.

Tanzimat Reforms

Young Ottomans

Abd al-Hamid II

Young Turks

Pic 848: What kinds of values and ideas from the European Enlightenment are on display in this image?

Secularization

Zooming In 850: After reading the selection, answer the analysis questions that follow:

1)

Matthew Perry

'Japanese Miracle'

Daimyo

Pic 854: Why did the 'Black Ships' from America help influence political change in Japan?

Meiji Restoration

Where did the new Meiji ruler claim descent from?	Give an example of Japan's adoption of Western technique or ideas in this era:

Fukuzawa Yukichi

Shinto

What kind of social changes did Kishida Toshiko argue for in Japanese society?	Evaluate: To what extent did society conform to her recommendations?

Zaibatsu

Infanticide

Pic 858: The U.S. Transcontinental Railroad was completed in 1869. How long before or after was this painting of a Japanese railroad released to the public?

____

Japan near the turn of the century fought and won two conflicts. Who were they fought against and when?

1) 2)

How was the Japanese victory over Russia specifically, the first time a non-European power had defeated a European power in a long time, seen by the following:

American strategists

Poles, Finns and Jews ruled by Russia

Chinese reformers

Islamic governments

Indonesian Muslims

Egyptian nationalists

Map 860: 1) Sketch the Japanese islands below, labeling the cities and placing the factories in the appropriate places. 2) Now sketch the Japanese territories of Korea and Taiwan, along with the Ryukyu Islands in the south and the Kuril Islands in the north.

Worst prediction of the century nominee: "This is the war to end all wars- that will make the world safe for democracy" – Woodrow Wilson

Pic 880: Do you get this joke? Here goes: "So, a Soviet soldier and the American soldier met in Germany at the end of WWII, after they jointly won the war. They even hugged for a photo-op. The American asked the Russian what the government told him he was fighting for. "They say we have to struggle for peace, always to struggle for peace," he said. "Hmm," the American mused, "Struggling for peace? Seems like a contradiction in terms, but whatever." Then the Russian asked him the same in return, "Why you fight?" And the American recalled seeing this WWI recruitment poster at his post office in New York state, which they put back in the window for WWII. He answered, "Well, we Americans will *always* fight for liberty- we have to, at least that's what they told us when I got drafted." The Russian's eyebrow raised, "So, even in America you have no choice but to fight, for the liberty to fight for liberty?" The American paused a moment and shrugged, "Yeah, well, something like that." America doesn't have conscription (the draft) anymore, but if it came back, and you were called up for, let's say, a war against Iran, what do you think you would do?

Christmas Truce

The 'Great War'

The 'Proud Tower'

Note the original three on each side at the outbreak of WWI:

Triple Alliance *Triple Entente*

Franz Ferdinand

Which country was promoting itself the leader of the Slavic nations and encouraging Slavic nationalism against the German-led empires?	Map 885: The three 'independent' countries in the Eastern Hemisphere were these:
List the 'novel' (new and interesting) weapons that the Industrial Age had produced by WWI:	Pic 887: What kinds of jobs did women like this one
Map 886: List the states that were neutral- not on either alliance- before WWI:	Describe the conditions for the soldiers in the trench warfare of the Western Front:

The Guns of August were hauled to battlefronts in mobilizations in many countries. Why do you think many young soldiers, brought up on stories about their ancestors' bravery and heroism in battle, got disillusioned by a war in which industrially made weapons sprayed bullets all over a battlefield, and living or dying was a matter of luck as much as anything else?

'Total war'

'War socialism'

All Quiet on the Western Front

For what social purpose did France begin the tradition of Mothers' Day after WWI?

What kind of new lifestyle did the 'flappers' of the postwar 1920s generation have that shocked their Victorian and Edwardian elders?

Note some of the new consumer goods that were becoming available to buy with the onset of electricity in homes:

Map 889: The three empires on the losing side, Germany, Austria-Hungary and Ottoman Turkey, were cut up into many new independent states on the principle of self-determination of nations. Still others were cut from Russia after it signed a separate peace treaty with Germany, which then lost the territory that was ceded. Which states were cut out of pieces of the following:

Austria-Hungary *Ottoman Turkey* *Germany/Russia*

National self-determination

What kind of conditions did the Treaty of Versailles place upon the losing side? Austria-Hungary and Ottoman Turkey were shorn of their empire, becoming Austria and Turkey respectively, while Germany was forced to do the following:

What did Hitler demand after hearing about the German surrender in WWI? ____________________

Armenian massacre ____

'Mandate' system ____

Instead of taking over Germany by force, like Lenin and Mussolini did in Russia and Italy, Hitler chose the 'path of legality.' But that meant he had to convince people to vote for him. He did this by giving antisemetic speeches which he developed a theory of why Germany surrendered. As a trench soldier, he saw the front firsthand, and believed Germany was still winning. Then he was injured at the Battle of the Somme, and later in a British Mustard Gas attack, after which he was sent to a military hospital. While there, Hitler heard about the surrender. How could it have happened? He blamed what he called the 'Jewish international world conspiracy,' and specifically German Jews, for 'stabbing Germany in the back,' pointing to the Balfour Declaration of 1917 as 'proof.' He put forth as true the conspiracy theory that 'Jews own all the banks,' as well as have command of the media and entertainment industries, through which they wield excessive influence over Western societies. Meanwhile, because the Bolshevik Party in Russia indeed had some leaders of Jewish origin, Hitler argued the entire communist revolution was, in fact, the Jewish takeover of Russia. Those same Russian Jews, Hitler argued further, were now sponsoring a Jewish-communist takeover of Germany. All this might have amounted to nothing, but after failing to get into art school in Vienna, Hitler joined a political party that was just starting up to fight the communists in Germany. Called the National Socialists, he believed this party would be the ticket to reversing the Versailles Treaty and exorcising, under a fascist order, all anti-German elements from the country. What kind of political environment did the combination of hyperinflation, the presence of the communist Red Guards, and popular anger over reparations related to the War Guilt Clause in the Versailles Treaty, create in the 1920s?

a. stable, most vote for centrist parties promising to keep things basically the same as they are

b. unstable, most vote for radical left and right parties promising to overturn the existing order

---

Why were the British in a unique position to influence policy in the Middle East, including Palestine and Transjordan, after WWI?

Fourteen Points ____

League of Nations ____

Collective Security ____

Black Thursday (10/24/29) ____

Great Depression ____

Snapshot 892: Unemployment hit a low in the USA in ____________, just before the Great Depression began. Which of the three countries maintained the lowest unemployment rate throughout the Great Depression?

____

The worst year for U.S. unemployment was:

The Nazi Party became more and more popular in Germany as conditions worsened. When they assumed control of the government on January 30, 1933, what happened to the unemployment situation in Germany?

Shantytowns

Just because there was a Great Depression going on didn't mean that Hollywood was going to stop making movies! In fact, *Superman* and other comic book heroes also arose in the 1930s, possibly to help feed a public desire for hope in the midst of the difficult economic times. Disney and Loony Tunes cartoons were becoming popular too. Place an appropriate check next to the major films of the decade:

	Seen it!	*Heard of it*	*Never even heard of it!*				
Our Daily Bread	_____	_____	_____	*Steamboat Willie*	_____	_____	_____
The Grapes of Wrath	_____	_____	_____	*Snow White*	_____	_____	_____
Mr. Deeds Goes to Town	_____	_____	_____	*Wizard of Oz*	_____	_____	_____
Mr. Deeds... Washington	_____	_____	_____	*Gone with the Wind*	_____	_____	_____
Meet John Doe	_____	_____	_____	*It's a Wonderful Life*	_____	_____	_____
Little Caesar	_____	_____	_____	*Why We Fight*	_____	_____	_____
The Public Enemy	_____	_____	_____	*Heard of any other movies from the '30s?*			
Gold Diggers	_____	_____	_____				
It Happened One Night	_____	_____	_____	________________________________			

The Great Depression: *a. affected the United States primarily* *b. affected many countries*

Describe the situation in the following countries that contributed to the mix of economic lolfails that led to the Great Depression:

United States	*Germany & Austria*	*Britain & France*

How did the following places become affected by the Great Depression?

Southeast Asia	*West Africa*	*Latin America*

Getulio Vargas

Lazaro Cardenas

Pic 894: What is your reaction to this famous image from *Life Magazine*?

'Democratic socialism'

Franklin D. Roosevelt

New Deal

John Maynard Keynes

Social Security

Minimum wage

Axis Powers

Fascism

What kinds of political ideas did fascists say weakened the nation and are, therefore, bad?

Benito Mussolini

Pic 897: Want to see what a *fasces* looks like? Mussolini isn't holding one here. It's a branch-wrapped ax carried by the Caesars in Roman times, now used as the symbol of Italian fascism and a reinvigorated consciousness of Roman history and power. It is an important symbol- it gave the term 'fascism' its name. If you want to see it, look no further than on the money of the time- American money! What? Oh yeah. *Image search: Mercury Head Dime*. This is what a dime looked like before the modern one. On the front, the Roman god Mercury, wings on his helmet, gazes into the distance, while on the back is a *fasces*- that classic symbol of America- err, rather, of authoritarian rule. During WWII, when American forces were fighting in Italy, troops no doubt had some of these dimes with this symbol of 'the enemy' on them (for perspective, imagine if the dime had a *Swastika* on it- the *fasces* wasn't much different). Before long, back on the homefront at the mint, it was decided, "Uh, we should probably take this ax thing off the money." So, after the war, they removed the Roman deity and replaced it with Franklin Roosevelt, and the *fasces* on the back became a 'torch of freedom,' which is still on the dime today. Check that one out if you have one in your pocket. Do you think symbols that acquire 'reputations' should be removed from circulation, or do you think the public has the maturity to say to itself, "Well we do have a *fasces* on our money, but it doesn't mean we are actually fascists." What other symbols does Mussolini have on his person that demonstrate power in this pic?

How about that 'other' symbol? Perhaps the world's most hated (or stigmatized) symbol, the *Hakenkreuz*, is shown here on Hitler's arm. It was chosen by him personally as the emblem of the 'revitalized German nation.' He chose it because it really was an ancient symbol of the Aryans, who he believed, like Gobineau, were the original Europeans. It is banned in Germany today, along with other NS symbols like *SS* flashes. In India, however, it is not only legal, but respected as a symbol of purity, harmony and nobility in Hinduism. Recall, way back in Ch. 4, a branch of European 'Aryans' brought it to India during the migrations millennia ago. Thus, it is still found there without stigma, although some detractors now view it as symbolic of the formerly institutionalized caste segregation, which was simultaneously a form of race segregation (*varnas*). In English, the *Hakenkreuz* is known as the:

a. Hooked Cross *b. Gammadion* *c. Swastika* *d. Weird X* *e. Stylized ICP Runner*

'Corporate state'

Lateran Accords

What country in Africa- one of only two that was still independent- did Italy invade to start a 'new Roman Empire?

After the Allies ended the German Empire and absorbed its colonies in Africa and Asia, they legislated for it a new democratic government called:

Freikorps

'The stab in the back'

Third Reich

What were some reasons the Nazis were so popular in Germany that they were democratically elected?

Note some of the restrictions the Nazi government placed on Jews after 1933:

Mein Kampf

Pic 900: Anti-Semitism is a term that indicates hatred, dislike and/or distain for people of Jewish origin. 'Semite' is an ethnic term for people of Middle Eastern background, such as ancient Hebrews and Arabs. Nazi propaganda, following Hitler's lead, labeled Jews as 'eternally' seeking to dominate Western societies such as Germany using whatever ideology would work best for that purpose at the time, no matter if it was 'right' or 'left' wing- 'capitalist' or 'communist.' What symbols of that kind of ideological duplicity are being used in this Anti-Semitic propaganda poster?

Kristallnacht

Nuremberg Laws

German family policy promoted: *a. abortion and contraception* *b. motherhood and more children*

National Socialist philosophy generally *a. agreed with* *b. opposed* Enlightenment ideals.

Fuhrer

What kinds of ideals was Japan absorbing from the European Enlightenment during the 1920s?

Moga

Mobo

'Rice riots'

Zooming In 902: After reading the selection, answer the analysis questions that follow:

1)

2)

3)

Pic 904: These women are wearing *a. indigenous* *b. imported* styles in this pic.

'National emergency'

Revolutionary Right

Cherry Blossom Society

What were the political goals of the Cherry Blossom Society?

'Resocialization'

While Authoritarian Japan did not produce a politician-figure like Mussolini and Hitler for people to rally behind, they already had someone who fulfilled that purpose. Who was that?	Describe the contents of the book *Cardinal Principles of the National Entity of Japan*:

Manchuria

Manchukuo

Note four reasons many Japanese felt their national survival was at stake by the late-1930s:

1) *2)*

3) *4)*

'Asia for Asians'

What happened on December 7, 1941?	For what reasons did Japan take this action?

Map 908: Note the timeframes for the following battles, row-by-row:

_________*Pearl Harbor* _________*Coral Sea* _________*Midway*

_________*Guadalcanal* _________*Guam* _________*Leyte Gulf*

_________*Iwo Jima* _________*Okinawa* _________*Hiroshima*

Lebensraum

Rhineland

Munich Conference

'Appeasement'

What happened on September 1, 1939?

In 1939, Britain and France declared war on Germany because Germany had invaded Poland over a disagreement about Danzig (Gdansk), access through the Polish Corridor, and the alleged treatment of German minorities living in Poland. Britain had an agreement with Poland, like the alliance system in WWI, because the British government had issued a war-guarantee to it, something they did not do for Czechoslovakia. This, guarantee, however, turned a local conflict into a much wider war. During the next six years, Poland lost ~6,000,000 of its citizens, was disassembled and divided between Nazi Germany and Soviet Russia, the people suffered untold privations, cultural genocide took place on a huge scale, and after the war, a war *won by Poland's allies,* it was subjected to communist domination against its will for the next 45 years. Seen in those terms, were British, Polish and other Allied objectives met at the end of this war?

Blitzkrieg

Map 911: Note the events that correspond to these *beginning* dates:

Sept. 1939: ________________________ *Fall, 1940:* ________________________

May, 1941: ________________________ *Sept. 1941:* ________________________

Dec. 1941: ________________________ *Summer '42:* ________________________

Aug. 1942: ________________________ *Nov. 1942:* ________________________

Nov. 1942: ________________________ *May, 1943:* ________________________

July, 1943: ________________________ *July, 1943:* ________________________

July, 1943: ________________________ *Aug. 1943:* ________________________

Sept. 1943: ________________________ *May, 1944:* ________________________

June, 1944: ________________________ *June, 1944:* ________________________

Aug. 1944: ________________________ *Dec. 1944:* ________________________

May, 1945: ________________________

Note the new technologies in WWII that accounted for many of the 60 million deaths:

Rape of Nanjing

Pic 912: One thing the textbook doesn't go into much is what happens to women during wartime, probably because it is not at all nice. When we read Genghis Khan is the direct ancestor of 16 million people living in Central Asia today, we realize it is only because his used mass rape as a weapon of war or reward for himself and his soldiers in every village and town he overran. Akbar the Mughal had 800 wives, and harems existed- and still do- across much of the world. The biggest form of slavery and human trafficking in modern times is of young women. In war, if the enemy army is not following 'civilized' rules of engagement, then you get what happened at Nanjing at the beginning of WWII, and at the end, with the mass rape of 2,000,000 European women by Soviet soldiers in 1945-1947. Now, like men, women and children faced a new threat in war. What kind of 'death from the sky' was used by both sides on civilians in enemy cities?

Zooming In 912: After reading the selection, answer the analysis questions that follow:

1)

Rosie the Riveter

Holocaust

Genocide

Have genocides as the UN has defined it occurred since the Second World War?

What did Winston Churchill- who believed in the British Empire and in imperialism- say that many people in the colonies took to mean the imperial idea was nearing an end?

Joseph Stalin

Victory Day

UN

World Bank / IMF

Which two victorious Allied Powers became world superpowers after the war? (circle both):

a. Great Britain *b. Soviet Union* *c. United States*

If the 16th was the Spanish century and the 17th the Dutch century, the 18th the French century, the 19th the British century and the 20th the American century, what do you think the 21st century might be called in the future?

Marshall Plan

NATO

Map 918: Note the countries that entered the EEC / European Union at the following times:

Original Members *1973-1986* *1990-2004*

'Brexit'

"I can't take anymore of this dang shopping!" -Worst thing for Anglophone tourist to yell in Beijing market during 1980s

Pic 928: This propaganda poster was released after Lenin died in 1924.

What does it say?	What does that mean or convey to the reader?	Why is the year on the poster there?

In Marxist theory, what is the final stage of historical development?	Describe the core beliefs of the ideology of Marxism:

Warsaw Pact

What 'mystique' did the communist movements of the 20th century borrow from the French Revolution of the 18th century?	Note the philosophies of the political parties guided by Marxism:

'Bread and Peace'

Nikolai II

'February Revolution'

Provisional Government

Bolsheviks

Lenin

'October Revolution'

Russian Civil War

USSR

Map 934: Leaving Moscow on the Trans-Siberian Railroad, which is the *first* large city one would come to that did *not* have Bolshevik activity going on in 1917:

a. Kazan *b. Omsk* *c. Novosibirsk* *d. Irkutsk* *e. Vladivostok*

The fact that Bolshevik activity was going on in Yerevan, Armenia and Tiflis, Georgia, tell us

a. that only Russians were interested in communism *b. that not only Russians were interested in communism*

Josef Stalin

Pic 936: See the black-lettered Russian Cyrillic writing on this poster?

Latin alphabet spelling= Kontr-Revolutsya *English meaning= Counter-Revolution*

This being the case, what do the following Cyrillic letters sound like in the English alphabet?

Н = **Р=** **В=** **л=**

ю= **ц=** **и=** **я=**

Josef Broz 'Tito'

Mao Zedong

CCP

Guomindang

Marriage Law

Pic 937: What inspired people in China about the Long March?

People's Liberation Army

The PLA was at war with the Chinese nationalists and the Japanese forces at the same time: *T* *F*

Map 939: Mao Zedong originated in the following area:

a. Beijing *b. Ji'an* *c. Shanghai* *d. Hong Kong*

It is correct to say that the Long March went north in a straight line: *T* *F*

The Japanese did not rule this area by 1938: *a. Manchuria* *b. Korea* *c. Sichuan*

There is a joke in communist societies about party members. It says, "We believe in equality, but some are more equal than others." What did CCP members have in China that non-party members did not?

'Totalitarian' measures

"Stalin called for the kulaks' liquidation." Indeed. *Democide,* 'death by government,' is when your *own government* kills you because you are politically incorrect or inconvenient to have around. Democide was rampant in the early Soviet Union. The Great Famine (1933), known in Ukraine as the *Holodomor,* is a good example. It began when the state collectivized agriculture and took food-as-tax from the peasants until millions starved and skeletal people wandered the countryside. More millions went to gulags. At the same time, the Soviet government presented an "everything is normal and prosperous" face to the outside world, by entertaining journalists like Walter Duranty on tours that would have made Potemkin blush. If such a social upheaval happened in your society and you were faced with the possibility of joining 'the bad guys' to save yourself and people close to you, If your government promised you a better life if you acted as a domestic spy, without telling anyone in your personal life that you were living this 'double-life,' would you consider the job? Why or why not?

What kinds of legislation affecting women and familial relationships did the communist governments enact?

Zhenotdel

What do the following communist slogans regarding women's issues mean, and to what extent to you agree with their message?

	"The traditional (husband-led) family must wither away"	*"Women can do anything"*
Meaning:		
My Opinion:		

Pic 941: While a guy rides in back, a woman drives this tractor- traditionally a man's job in Russia- on a collective farm. How was a collective farm different than a privately-owned farm?

In China, former landowners and factory managers were shamed in public by their former tenants and employees, by being yelled at in front of a large crowd of peasants and/or workers. If you had the chance to yell at someone in authority over you now and get away with it because all the 'rules' got flipped and now you were the boss, would you take advantage of the opportunity- or would you rather not mess with the existing social structure in your country?

Kulaks

'People's communes'

One thing the communists in Russia and China did well was:

a. increase personal freedoms *b. increase industrial output and educational standards*

Snapshot 944: Select three items from this list that are most shocking or surprising to you and explain why you chose them:

Rationale

1)

2)

3)

Great Leap Forward

Cultural Revolution

'Iron girls'

Pic 945: This poster is promoting the new economic prosperity, but what is it hiding?

If there was a giant crime wave in your country and the media wasn't reporting on it, might you think something weird was going on?

Magnitogorsk

If you were a lawyer arguing in a court case prosecuting the communist regimes of the Cold War for environmental destruction, select three pieces of evidence you would enter:

Exhibit A:

Exhibit B:

Exhibit C:

The Great Purge

Gulags

Red Guards

Was the Iron Curtain really a curtain?

What was it built to separate?

Zooming In 948: After reading the selection, answer the analysis questions that follow:

1)

Note the background of the conflicts in the following places during the Cold War:

	Korea	*Vietnam*	*Afghanistan*
Timeframe:			
Background:			

Map 950: List the Cold War crisis areas in each of the AP World History world regions:

Latin America	*Europe*	*Middle East*	*Africa*
South Asia	*East Asia*	*Southeast Asia*	*Other*

Fidel Castro

Nikita Khrushchev

JFK

Cuban Missile Crisis

Pic 953: Beautifully terrifying, the mushroom cloud became a staple obsession of the Cold War. From the *Terminator* movies to the themes of annihilation in heavy metal music during the 1980s, it wasn't immediately clear that *Mutually Assured Destruction (MAD)* would take place if enough nukes were launched at the same time, and the fact that Carl Sagan and other scientists didn't yet release the information before the Cuban Missile Crisis is a bit scary. Hopefully by the time you read this, Hiroshima and Nagasaki will still be the only two populated areas ever hit with atom bombs. Are they?

Zooming In 955: After reading the selection, answer the analysis questions that follow:

1)	*Cuban*	*Russian*	*Chinese*
Similarities			
Differences			

'Military-Industrial Complex'

Which currency did the U.S. dollar replace during the Cold War as the GRC (Global Reserve Currency)?

Note the types of American pop culture and consumer goods that became worldwide phenomena during the period of American superpower stardom during the Cold War decades:

Music	*Fast Food*	*Brand Names*	*English Global Slang*

Pic 957: Finally, some actual color pictures! Okay the nuke was in color. During which of the following attempts at reforming or getting rid of communism was this picture taken?

a. The 1956 Hungarian Uprising in Budapest *b. The 1968 Prague Spring in Czechoslovakia*

What was the goal of this concept of 'socialism with a human face?'	What was the Soviet response to these demands?

'Triangular diplomacy'

'Miracle year'

Describe the collapse of hard communism in its power centers in the 'three acts':

Act I	*Act II*	*Act III*

On December 25, 1991, the whole world got a Christmas present. What was it?

Deng Xiaoping

'Literature of the wounded'

Pic 960: Is China a communist country still? Technically yes, because it is still a one-party state under the political control of the CCP. But does it have a communist command economy? Note some things that make China suspiciously not seem very much like a communist *society*:

Tiananmen Square massacre

Perestroika

Glasnost

Describe the effects of *Glasnost* on Soviet society:

Mikhail Gorbachev

How did Chernobyl's meltdown and the Berlin Wall's destruction affect people psychologically?	What does Vladimir Putin not want NATO to do now, almost 30 years after Cold War's end?

The nice thing about one-party states is that you don't have to spend all that time researching the issues and candidates before voting

Pic 974: Does this school in South Africa have a dress code that includes uniforms? ____________

The 'Global South' is the newest perhaps rather odd name that 'First Worlders' seem to want to give to 'Everyone Else.' A century ago you had the 'civilized world' and the 'uncivilized world,' and one of the justifications for colonialism, recall, was to 'civilize' the uncivilized. During colonial times before 1960, then, the poorer part of the world was thought of simply 'the colonies.' But that would change after the worldwide movement to end imperial rule, and a new way of describing the world was required. That's when the Cold War divisions of First, Second and Third World came into vogue. The First World was the 'free and prosperous' world of North America, Western Europe, Australia, New Zealand and perhaps Japan. Maybe Israel and South Africa too. The Second World was the communist world of the Soviet Union and Eastern Europe- all the stuff behind the Iron Curtain. Everything else was the Third World. And it was poor. In the 1980s and 1990s, when the Second World was moving away from communism, geographers switched descriptive names to the 'developed' and 'undeveloped' worlds, but soon 'undeveloped' was switched again to 'developing,' to make it seem like the undeveloped world had some action going on, and some of the places might become 'developed' at some point. Besides, isn't every country 'developing' in some way? Then, it became MDCs and LDCs, or else, 'more developed' and 'less developed' countries. Not much different. After 2000, geographers noticed that during colonial times and the Cold War, it was always countries in the northern latitudes that were doing the dominating, so they changed Third World and 'Developing World' to 'The Global South.'

In your opinion, is it a good term? Why or why not?	Is Australia part of it?	Is there a goal or end point we are supposed to be developing to?

The countries of the former colonial world that achieved independence in the 1940s were:

'Pacific Way' ________________

Just so we're clear on this, define again the term national *self-determination*:

Which of the following did not present a philosophical challenge to European governments that ruled colonial holdings overseas?

a. Christian heritage *b. Enlightenment thought* *c. Social darwinist arguments*

Map 980: List the African states that became independent in each of the following decades:

1940s	*1950s*
1960s	*1970s*
1980s	*1990s*

Map 981: List the Asian and Middle Eastern states that- like Iraq in 1932- became independent in each of the following decades:

1940s	*1950s*
1960s	*1970s*
1980s	*1990s*

Who are considered the 'fathers' of the following countries:

India:	*Indonesia:*	*Vietnam:*
Ghana:	*South Africa:*	*United States:*

Guerrilla warfare

Before modern times, most people in India thought of themselves as 'Indians': *T* *F*

Indian National Congress

'Babus'

Mohandas Gandhi

Pic 984: The simple garment Gandhi is known for wearing was called a ____________.

Answer a few questions about Gandhi's biography:

Indian state he was born in:

Caste of his family:

Age he was married:

Was he a great student:

Country he got to study in:

Profession he worked for:

Country he moved to in 1893:

Why he didn't like it there:

Satyagraha

Year he returned to India:

Party he joined in India:

Why people liked him:

Mahatma

How he felt about modern society:

How he argued women could help:

Jawaharlal Nehru

When Nehru was in Naini jail for anti-British activism in the 1930s, he wrote a world history book to his daughter, the future Indira Gandhi, as a series of letters. They have since been collected and published as *Glimpses of World History,* a forerunner to your textbook. Indira studied Malthus, diseases and famines of the past. She enacted a population control law that forcibly tied the tubes of women and gave vasectomies to men. Do you agree or disagree that if a country's population gets too high or grows too fast, that the state should get into people's personal decisions at this level 'for the good of society'?

Bande Mataram

Urdu

Muhammad Ali Jinnah

How many people were ethnically cleansed from Pakistan to India and vice-versa during the separation of the two countries? | How many died *en route* or of communal violence?

Did Gandhi's dream come true? If you were a lawyer arguing both sides, what would be your primary points in discussing the following:

Gandhi's dream did come true | *Gandhi's dream did not come true*

Map 987: The areas of Northern India that are still in dispute to this day are:

a. Sri Lanka and Bengal *b. Jammu and Kashmir* *c. Gujarat and Assam*

After South Africa was independent in 1910, the percentage of people who were white was:

Afrikaners

Can there really be 'white Africans'? The *Afrikaners* believed being a 'white African' was not a contradiction in terms, and that they were exactly that because they identified themselves based on the name of the land they lived in since the 1600s, which, recall, is about the same time the Pilgrims came to America. A book written about the *Afrikaners* in the 1980s even called them *The White Tribe of Africa.* So, in your opinion, can they choose to identify that way? Some black Africans think they shouldn't be allowed to. Conversely, in your opinion, can there be black Europeans, or Asian Africans like Gandhi when he lived in South Africa? Come to think of it, can there really be 'white Americans?' Pick a position and expound:

Can there be a 'white African'? | 'Can there be a 'black European'? | Can there really be a 'white American'?

Zooming In 988: After reading the selection, answer the analysis questions that follow:

1)

2)

Dr. H.F. Verwoerd designed the South African segregation system, called *apartheid.* He justified it under the assumption that different races would not cooperate if they voted in the same democratic elections, arguing they would simply compete with each other, and whichever race held the majority would always dominate the others with their voting power- and that that was the weakness of democracy. His *apartheid* policy split the country into a white area governed by 'white supremacy,' meaning only whites could be citizens and vote, and ten tribal reserves for groups like the Xhosa, Zulu and Tswana, governed by 'black supremacy' and tribal law. Large cities in the white area of the country could have black and Asian residents, but they would be citizens of a tribal reserve, not of the Republic of South Africa, and their neighborhoods would be segregated. To get to the white part of the city, blacks, coloureds (an official census term for 'mixed') and Asians needed a special pass card, and when they were there, they were not allowed to use the same facilities as whites, like in the American South before the Civil Rights Act of 1964. That act outlawed 'white' and 'colored' drinking fountains, movie theaters, beaches, restaurants, and so forth, but segregation under *apartheid* continued in South Africa another 30 years, until 1994. But why go to all this trouble? The tide of history was clearly against South Africa during those decades. Why do you think the whites of the country- 10% of the population- so afraid of regular majority-rules democratic elections?

____

'Pass laws' ____

'Bantustan' ____

ANC ____

National Party ____

Nelson Mandela ____

Pic 991: A rising star in the African National Congress, Mandela co-created a 'militant arm' of the party called *Umkhonto w Sizwe* (Spear of the Nation) whose goal it was to fight the white-dominated government of South Africa until they allowed blacks to vote in majority-rules national elections. In order to attract fighters to join, he gave the famous speech quoted at the beginning of this chapter on pg. 975, saying he would be 'ready to die' fighting the white government of Dr. Verwoerd. Mandela sent a letter to the government in 1961 threatening trouble if the whites would not hold a constitutional convention and rewrite the laws. They didn't, and Mandela's group began a wave of attacks on power plants, electricity substations and other utility facilities- 193 in all. *Umkhonto w Sizwe* was labeled a terrorist organization by the government, and Mandela was arrested, put on trial, found guilty and sentenced to life in prison. What is Mandela shown doing in this picture, 30-years later?

____

The police have a tough job in any country, but in South Africa, race was the biggest issue on everyone's mind. Around 150 white police were facing a crowd of ~10,000 black protesters, who the police said were armed with machetes and pipe bombs. They claimed the crowd was going to overrun and maul them, so they opened fire to drive back the crowd. It worked, but the crowd kept coming and they kept firing. It was a horrible massacre, with international repercussions. The massacre turned the world's eyes to the racial divisions in South Africa, and South African teams were banned from the Olympics and other international sporting events as long as they only allowed white players to be on the national team. For perspective's sake, Jackie Robinson 'broke the color barrier' becoming the black player in the Major Leagues, in 1947, which was 13 years before Sharpeville. How many activists did the police kill at the massacre?

____

Black Consciousness

Soweto

Inkatha Freedom Party

Gatsha Buthelezi

Map 992: Names on a map tell about changing circumstances. The purple inset map shows four provinces in the days of apartheid. What are they?

1) *2)* *3)* *4)*

When the new ANC government took over in 1994, one of the first things they did was begin changing the names of places in the country to reflect African- instead of white- heroes and things. The province of Transvaal, an Afrikaner name, was broken up into four sections, three of which were renamed with African words, and the fourth with an English word. What are they?

1) *2)* *3)* *4)*

Currently, there is a big debate in South Africa about the name of the capital city, which is Pretoria, but which the government wants to change to an African name: Tshwane. Andrius Pretorius, for whom the capital was named, was a hero to the white Afrikaners in the 1800s. Who do you think should have the right to change names? Should it be a vote, or should the government decide?

The fact that apartheid ended without a 'racial bloodbath' was: *a. surprising* *b. expected*
(although there almost was- Youtube: *Terreblanche The Whites' Last Stand* to see)

Kwame Nkrumah

How much of the world's population was, is or will be African and Asian in the following years?

1950: *2000:* *2050:*

Snapshot 994: Summarize the level of population growth in the following regions between 1970 and 2011:

North America:	*a. significant growth*	*b. not much growth*
Europe:	*a. significant growth*	*b. not much growth*
Latin America:	*a. significant growth*	*b. not much growth*
Africa:	*a. significant growth*	*b. not much growth*
Asia:	*a. significant growth*	*b. not much growth*

Two regions are not only not growing, but losing population (they don't seem to be shrinking, but that is only because their numbers are maintained by immigration from other world regions). Which two regions do you think these are (hint: you probably live in one)?

Congress Party

What do the authors mean when they say, "In many parts of the world, democracy had been a fragile transplant?

Do you think every country should have a democratic government? The U.S. had been trying to bring democracy to many countries like Iraq, but it has proven difficult. Should that policy continue?

One negative consequence of the end of European colonial rule in Africa has been:

a. more jobs *b. free markets expanding* *c. more tribal warfare*

Pic 997: What social fact about Brazil does this famous picture of Sao Paulo depict?

Aprista Movement

Juan Peron

Salvador Allande

Zooming In 998: After reading the selection, answer the analysis questions that follow:

1)

2)

Augusto Pinochet

Beginning in 2011 with the 'Arab Spring,' many longstanding Middle Eastern dictators, like Mubarak of Egypt, Gadhafi of Libya, and possibly soon Bashar al-Assad of Syria have been toppled by popular demonstrations. What kinds of values to the authors believe the demonstrators demanding change have been asking for?

Vladimir Putin of Russia polls at an 80% favorability among Russian voters, other presidents who are less authoritarian generally poll 50% or less. In your opinion, is authoritarian rule always bad?

Arab Spring

'Development economics'

'State capitalism'

How did the development strategy differ in Latin America and East Asia?

'Urban bias'

'Male bias'

'Human capital'

Snapshot 1004: How many cities in the top 20 were in North America and Europe (including USSR/Russia) in the following:

1950: *2014:*

In 2014, write the names of the cities in the top 20 under the appropriate headings:

North America *Latin America* *Europe*

Africa *Middle East* *Asia*

Pic 1005: What is a 'microloan' and what is the benefit of using that system, if any?

As you probably know, modern American/Western culture is driven hard by the mass media. Moguls and focus groups pick out the next big stars, big songs, big fashions, and big values-issues, and then relentlessly promote them across all channels and online, until we are forced by our participation in public discourse to take a position. No matter what position we take, however, we are interacting with has been *chosen for us*. *Click. Like.* When you *Like* something, you know what they do with that data? Now those same moguls are exporting *their* decisions worldwide, and the world is fooled into thinking what they are exporting is your culture, *our culture,* when it is actually that of the media empire. Think about that. They want people to believe *you and me* are overspreading our culture around the world destroying others. Is that true? If so, shaming us for it might be something we need to hear, but it may not be. To find out, ask yourself this: How do you relate to- or how much do you like, or believe in, or associate with- global pop culture? Before answering remember that you might be speaking from *inside* the world of pop culture, and don't necessarily see it around you, and your role in it, just as we cannot see the Milky Way Galaxy because we are inside of it. Try to get some distance for a moment. Step back from it all, and look at your values and what you like from the outside. See it for what it really is. Alright, how do you relate to- or how much do you like, or believe in, or associate with- the following phenomena, all of which clash with various cultural norms around the world:

Feminism:

Rock:

Rap:

Sexual permissiveness:

Consumerism:

Democracy:

As modernity clashes with traditional cultures around the world in our time, do you have a good answer for the following people?

I am an African medicine man, and I don't believe in Western medicine. What do I do to compete with those foreign doctors in the tent down the road? My people are seeing them now.

I am a Chinese grandfather, and it disturbs me that my apartment building is now dominated by young people and their music. Can I ask them to turn it down?

I am a Muslim woman in Syria, and see American women on TV all the time. Why don't I have the same rights & freedoms they do? Are European values really universal, or not?

Ataturk

Why is Ataturk often compared with Peter I the Great?

Pic 1007: What were Ataturk's beliefs about how a country like Turkey could and should modernize?

Today, the reforms of Ataturk a century ago are *a. still in effect* *b. being rescinded in part*

Why was Iran an unlikely place for an Islamist revolution when the Shah ruled in the 1970s?

White Revolution ______

Ayatollah ______

Ruhollah Khomeini ______

Council of Guardians ______

What did Ayatollah Khomeini believe the purpose of government was?

Note some of the things done in 1980 in the interests of creating an Islamic state in Iran:	How did women's lives change under the Ayatollah's reforms?

Farsi ______

Hijab ______

Pic 1009: Whatever you do, don't Youtube: *Naked Gun Gorbachev* to see the Ayatollah. What is the current status of Iran?

Don't worry- the future looks bright. Think positive! Now let's all do jumping-jacks together as a class.

Pic 1022: *Spaceship Earth* is a motif of thought invented by Buckminster Fuller, who worked with Walt Disney on that giant silver golf ball-looking thing at Epcot. Consider this image of the Earth in conjunction with the exchange between the President of the United States and the first astronauts on the moon, as they spoke to each other across the space between the two objects in this picture:

Transcript of the Telephone Call from the White House to the Moon:

President Nixon: *"Hello, Neil and Buzz... because of what you have done, the heavens have become a part of man's world. And as you talk to us from the Sea of Tranquility, it inspires us to redouble our efforts to bring peace and tranquility to Earth. For one priceless moment in the whole history of man, all the people on this Earth are truly one; one in their pride in what you have done, and one in our prayers that you will return safely to Earth."*

Neil Armstrong: *"Thank you, Mr. President. It's a great honor and privilege for us to be here representing not only the United States but men of peace of all nations... with interest, curiosity and vision for the future."*

There is an anomaly in your textbook. In a book about the history of the world, they somehow forgot to put a page or two about the people who left the world and went to another one. Actually, they left out the exploration of space altogether. Why? Only they know. Look in the index and try to find Armstrong, Neil or Aldrin, Buzz, the first people to walk on a world *other* than the one you see on Pg. 933. The mission's name was *Project Apollo*. Some say it was humanity's greatest achievement. Adjusted for inflation, the entire program including all the research and development of products and equipment, all the training, and the six landings, cost 110 billion dollars. A similar program of a mission to Mars is estimated by NASA to cost about the same, over ten years' time. On the other hand, the wars in the Middle East since Sept. 11th have cost 1,700 billion dollars, as of 2016. If America didn't have to deal with that, or chose not to, about how many times could we have already established a human presence on Mars, even assuming no economies of scale, and that each mission would be 110 billion while the wars cost 1,700 billion?

____

Do you think that would be a better option? Why or why not?

Bretton Woods

Describe how Foreign Direct Investment (FDI) works:

Map 1027: Rate the following countries in order of how much FDI they obtained in the late-20th century: Australia, Brazil, Canada, China, Great Britain, Japan, Russia, USA:

1

2

3

4

5

6

7

8

How is a TNC different than a regular corporation?

While made in the United States for the first 30 years of its production life, the Barbie doll by Mattel- now a TNC- is made in here these days:

Pic 1028: It's kind of a joke now that all tech support and call centers are based in India, so how are these workers making fun of the joke that they need to always be happy on the job?

Out of the top 100 economies in the world, how many are:

Countries: *Corporations:*

The Muslim-Hindu exchange following independence from Britain in India wasn't the first such ethnic cleansing operation in modern times. When the Armenian Genocide/Massacre was going on in Turkey during WWI, another mass migration was being prompted by the Turks against the Greek population of Anatolia, which had been living there for thousands of years. Around 500,000 Greeks were murdered by the Turks, while over a million Greeks escaped- some by swimming to U.S. ships waiting in the harbor after their historic city of Smyrna was purposefully burned- and headed to Greece proper. Where did Jews *not* migrate to as their presence in Central Europe was officially fought by the German government?

a. United States *b. Israel* *c. Greece*

Is imperialism still going on by another name? There are no European empires in African anymore, but how many Chinese have arrived to take control of large sections of the African economy?

'Labor migrant'

Many people have moved from: *a. urban to rural areas* *b. rural to urban areas* worldwide.

From which countries have most migrants to the following come from?

To Great Britain:

To France:

To Germany:

To United States:

Aside from the 12,000,000 or so illegal immigrants, how many legal immigrants has the United States allowed to enter the country since the Hart-Cellar Act of 1965 began a legal migrant flow?

'Coyote'

France has a reputation for being a land of liberty like the United States, but as the authors write, there is now a controversy about banning girls from wearing headscarves in school, because the ethnic French have gotten defensive about their values in opposition to large numbers of Muslim immigrants from North Africa, who often themselves defend wearing the headscarves in school. So what do you think? Should the Arabic girls be 'free' to wear the traditional dress in school, or should the French norms be followed in French schools?

Does humanity have anything to be proud about during the 21st century? What with the wars and poverty that exists- use evidence from the textbook to argue that humanity has at least *one thing* to be proud about in this century:

'Bubble of 2008'

Is 'equality' something worth striving for? Or should everyone take care of themselves?

In the last half of the 20th century, there was an east/west conflict that in the 21st has become a north/south conflict. What is the engine keeping the new conflict going?

George Soros

Who is George Soros and why is he mentioned in the book? You probably won't need to know him for the test, but knowing who he is might be worthwhile because he played such a large role as a foil to Donald Trump. Soros is a driving force promoting immigration of Middle Easterners to Europe and America, using his fortune to get politicians to agree to allowing more settlement of refugees. About this idea, Soros said the following, "Our plan treats the protection of migrants as the objective and national borders as the obstacle," meaning that countries don't mean anything and everything has to be decided as far as what is in the best interest of the migrants, not the people of the country they are trying to enter. This was a big voting issue in the 2016 U.S. presidential election, and President Trump called out Soros (who now lives in the U.S.) as someone who shouldn't enact his plan for more migration. Do you agree with Soros that countries should not have borders, and that migration should increase, or with Trump who says borders should be strengthened and migration should be lowered?

Snapshot 1031: Only one sex of people in one kind of country have a life expectancy over 80 years. Who are they?

A person in a low income country is about ___ times more likely to die of an infectious disease than you are.

a. 10 *b. 5* *c. 2*

How many people as a percentage of the population have access to toilets in the following places:

Low income countries	*Lower-middle income*	*Upper-middle income*	*Upper income*
____________	____________	____________	____________

Chiapas Rebellion

Anti-Globalization

What do anti-globalists around the world generally take as the basic tenants of their movement?

Do you think neoliberal globalization is a positive good or something to be discarded?

'Empire of production'

'Soft power'

Sept. 11, 2001

Saddam Hussein

'Terrorism'

Map: Is there any correlation between the number of McDonalds' in a country and the fact there is a military base there?

Map 1034: Does this map lie? The bubble that shows the number of McDonalds restaurants by country are not accurate. Look at the key. 10,000+ means the number in America is nearly the same size on the map as the number in Japan and China, and perhaps Britain and Germany, which, really, have only slightly above 2,000. Here are the stats (2016):

USA	14,267
Japan	2,975
China	2,050
Germany	1,477
Canada	1,429
France	1,325
Great Britain	1,240
Australia	930
Brazil	812
Russia	553
Italy	530
Philippines	500
Spain	496
South Korea	415
Taiwan	413
Mexico	402
Poland	370
Malaysia	314
Turkey	260
Netherlands	252

Using this information, draw the bubbles in the areas they would be in the world, with more precise relative sizes than they are on the map in the book:

Al-Qaeda

In 2014, Russia reacted against Ukraine and Georgia incorporating into NATO by doing what?

'Cultural imperialism'

Kyoto Protocol

Pic 1037: If you go to college, you'll certainly see Che's face, who has been adopted as a revolutionary hero. Do you think he is a hero? Pick a position and expound:

Simone de Beauvoir

Betty Friedan

Freedom Trashcan

Did black women latch on to the feminist movement, or did they consider it a battle between 'white women and white men?'

The first wave of the feminist movement in the 1920s was about gaining political power through voting. The second wave of the 1960s was about gaining social equality. The third wave, going on now, is about women in the non-Western world. What are the goals for women worldwide?

"Woman Question"

Pic 1041: Machismo is a Latin American standard of behavior for men. What have these women done to protest this 'manliness' attitude?

Modernity as a social phenomenon is usually thought to be 'bad' for organized religion. Why to you think that is?

Yet, religion has seen a resurgence in the West- but which religion, and why?

What did Christian minister Francis Schaeffer fear in his exposition on modern society?

Hindutva

BJP

Fundamentalism

What issues did the Muslim world have that by the 1970s began attracting people to become fundamentalist?

What is the role of Israel in attracting people to become fundamentalist?

Sayyid Qutb

Zooming In 1046: After reading the selection, answer the analysis questions that follow:

1)

2)

The West is always criticized for 'materialism.' What is that, to you?

Map 1048: List three countries that have the following percentages of Muslims:

	More than 90%	*75-90%*	*2-9%*	*Less than 2%*
1)				
2)				
3)				

Hamas ______________________________

Hezbollah ______________________________

Osama bin Laden ______________________________

Al-Qaeda ______________________________

Fatwa ______________________________

Salaf ______________________________

Wahhabism ______________________________

Pic 1050: Which other group did Hamas begin as a spinoff from? ______________________________

Late Pope John Paul II was asked if national feelings or patriotism had any place in the modern world and in the Christian heart. He said they did. He said patriotism is revealed to us as a properly ordered social love- an extension of the 4th Commandment (Honor thy Father and thy Mother) *back in time*, through the honoring of the land itself, understood as the spiritual patrimony which we acquire from our mother and father, as they acquired it from theirs, and so on, from time immemorial. In this way, he said:

"Society transcends materialism with a force that may be called 'spiritual capital,' that acts both as a regulator of the everyday, and the invisible glue that gives a society that little extra something, when times are tough and the political center does not hold. Patria is associated with the idea and reality of 'fatherhood,' or 'parenthood,' in the sense of caring for the land and making of it an 'enchanted homeland' over time. The native land can be identified as this patrimony, that is, something that is the totality of goods given down us by our forefathers... our native land is thus our heritage. It refers to the land, the territory, but more importantly, the concept of patria also includes the values and spiritual content that makes up the culture of a given nation."

According to John Paul II, what is the value of having a *country*?

Anthropocene ______________________________

'One Child' ______________________________

Mass extinction ______________________________

How have the following been shaped by human hands?

Lake Erie *Great Pacific Garbage Patch* *Atmospheric CO2*

____

Environmentalism

John Muir

Silent Spring

Limits to Growth

Small is Beautiful

Three Gorges Dam

Zooming In 1058: After reading the selection, answer the analysis questions that follow:

1)

Reforestation

Pic 1060: Where are these masked people and what are they protesting?

"One World" thinking seems to mean that you, as an individual, should look out for the world at-large, but as human people, we are in some ways constrained by 'who' we are on the global stage. We are people who embrace various 'isms' to define ourselves. How do you define yourself- what exactly *are* you?

Crash Course* Guide

Cobra ____________________

It's Review Time!

Topic of today's episode ______________________________________

Why was "Me From the Past's" question silly (or smart)?

____

What topic did "Thought Bubble" portray in this episode?

____

What did Mr. Green find in the "Secret Compartment?" ______________

Who (or what) was the "Open Letter" directed to? ____________________

How did that item tie in to the material in the chapter?

____

____

____

Was there a 'deep' lesson at the very end? What was it?

____

Any further notes you think are important:

*The producers of Crash Course were not involved in the production of this review worksheet.

History Movie Review

Reviewer ____________________

What chapter in the book is this movie most appropriate for? __________________________

The topic(s) it cover(s): ____

Identify some of the key characters in the movie / documentary that embody concepts in the chapter. Describe how the historical issue(s) affect the storyline in the early part of the film.

____

____

____

____

What was the "low point" or crisis for the main character(s) in the movie? How did the historical issue cause or influence that low point / crisis to occur?

____

____

By the end of the movie, it is probable that whatever crises or effects the historical issue was causing was resolved in some way. Explain how this turn of events came about:

____

____

____

Rate this movie from 0-3: ______________

3: it was intellectually stimulating and entertaining
2: it had good points but was rather dull
1: it seemed misleading or irrelevant
0: it was not worth seeing- waste of time

One image or scene that stuck out was:

____

____

____

Why did you rate it the way you did?

____

____

Would you recommend this movie to friends or relatives outside of history class?

____

____

Test Correction Guide

Corrector________________________

Time to get it right!

Test Name________________________

Directions: Identify the numbers of the answers you got wrong on the test and write them:

Number	**Page in Book**	**Correct answer (written in the form of a statement using stem of question)**

I got most of these wrong because…

100 Years of World History Textbooks

The subject of World History has changed a lot in the past century, since H.G. Wells wrote *The Outline of History* after the not so great Great War. Like everyone, he was in shock, and believed a history of 'all of us,' as one, which could be taught in schools in every country, accompanying the national history course, could facilitate greater cross-cultural understanding. Wells was a big-picture kind of writer, as were H.W. Van Loon (who won the first Newbery Award for his world history), and William McNeill, who helped craft the bases for the current AP World History curriculum fifty years later. Their successors have carried on this mantle.

Wells, H.G., *The Outline of History,* 1919
Webster, Hutton, *World History,* 1921
Van Loon, Hendrik, *The Story of Mankind,* 1921
Breasted, James, *The Conquest of Civilization,* 1926
Robinson, James, *The Ordeal of Civilization,* 1926
McKinley, Albert, *World History Today,* 1927
Thorndike, Lynn, *Short History of Civilization,* 1928
Parsons, Geoffrey, *The Stream of History,* 1928
Hayes, Carleton, *World History,* 1932
Nehru, Jawaharlal, *Glimpses of World History,* 1934
Barnes, Harry Elmer, *History of Civilization,* 1935
Gombrich, E.H., *A Little History of the World,* 1936
Heckel, A.K., *On the Road to Civilization,* 1937
Pahlow, Edwin, *Man's Great Adventure,* 1938
Hammerton & Barnes, *Illustrated World History,* 1940
Becker, Carl, *Story of Civilization,* 1946
Lane et al., *The World's History,* 1947
Rogers, Lester, *Story of Nations,* 1949
Muzzey, David S., *Struggle for Cvilization,* 1955
Brinton, Crane, *History of Civilization,* 1955
Starr, Chester, *History of the World,* 1960
Cole, Fay-Cooper, *Illustrated Outline of Mankind,* 1963
Braudel, Fernand, *History of Civilization,* 1963
Stavrianos, Leften, *Global History of Man,* 1963
McNeill, William, *The Rise of the West,* 1963
Neill, Thomas P., *Story of Mankind,* 1968
Garraty, John A., *Columbia History of the World,* 1972
Burns, Edward M., *World Civilizations,* 1974
Toynbee, Arnold, *Mankind and Mother Earth,* 1976
Ostrowski, Richard, *Echoes of Time,* 1977
Perry, Marvin, *Unfinished Journey,* 1980
Leinwand, Gerald, *Pageant of World History,* 1986
Asimov, Isaac, *Chronology of World History,* 1991
Gonick, Larry, *Cartoon History of the World,* 1991
Krieger, Larry, *Perspectives on the Past,* 1992
Roberts, J.M., *History of the World,* 1993

In use as AP World texts

Bentley et al., *Traditions and Encounters*
Bulliet et al., *The Earth and its Peoples*
Fernandez-Armesto, *The World*
Goucher et al., *Journeys from Past to Present*
Hansen et al., *Voyages in World History*
Lockard, *Societies, Networks and Traditions*
McKay et al., *A History of World Societies*
Reilly, *The Human Journey*
Smith et al., *Crossroads and Cultures*
Spodek, *The World's History*
Stearns et al., World Civilizations
Strayer, *Ways of the World*
Tignor et al., *Worlds Together, Worlds Apart*
Von Sivers et al., *Patterns of World History*

These are a sampling- other books
are used for on-level courses

Schur, Nathan, *Relevant History of the World,* 1997
Blainey, Geoffery, *A Short History of the World,* 2000
David, James C., *The Human Story,* 2004
Christian, David, *Maps of Time,* 2004
Brinkley et al., *National Geographic Visual History,* 2005
Lascelles, Christopher, *Short History of the World,* 2014

For more on the history of world history writing since ancient times, please do consult ***Universal History and the Telos of Human Progress* (2014)** by David Tamm on *Amazon,* which covers these historians and more.

Thank You!

If this resource book has no use for you, it has no value. We strive to make materials you can actually *use.* No waste, no filler, only usable resources with minimal marginalia aligned with the course for convenience. This is how *Tamm's Textbook Tools* works:

Coursepak A*,* the *Assignments* series has daily book-based guided readings for homework or in class. It has the vocab, people and chapter work covered, along with some application and subjective questions.

Coursepak B*,* The *Bundle* series of bell-ringers, warm ups and openers, available on *Amazon* and elsewhere, has material to be used as grabbers at the beginning of an hour, along with reading comp., online activities if students have computer time, multimedia and video clip response forms, short answers, and tickets-out-the-door. Look for the **AP World History** *Bundle* coursepak for Strayer 3rd specifically.

Coursepak C*,* The *Competencies* and *Crossovers* series, is the part of the *Tamm's Textbook Tools* line that goes into more depth on the one hand (competency) and stretches out to connect the disciplines (crossover). If you teach World History, for example, and want a history of the great moments and big ideas in the development of human cultures, or if you want to get an integrated curriculum crossover going with English, Math, Science, Fine Arts, Foreign Languages, or another department of the school, a *Coursepak C: Competencies and Crossovers* might be what you're looking for.

Look for these and more in the *Tamm's Textbook Tools* series, a low-cost, timesaving way to find high quality, custom materials tailor made to textbooks in many different subjects. Contact the marketing department anytime with suggestions, corrections and any other correspondence at hudsonfla@gmail.com. Find *TTT* on Facebook as well. Please inform your colleagues of the existence of this series if you think it will benefit them. Thank you!

Made in the USA
Lexington, KY
18 January 2019